# KEEP WATCH WITH ME

*An Advent Reader
for Peacemakers*

CLAIRE BROWN &
MICHAEL T. McRAY

Abingdon Press / Nashville

# Keep Watch with Me
An Advent Reader for Peacemakers

**Library of Congress Control Number has been requested.**
978-1-5018-7633-2

19 20 21 22 23 24 25 26 27 28 — 10 9 8 7 6 5 4 3 2 1
MANUFACTURED IN THE UNITED STATES OF AMERICA

*For all those*
*waiting, watching, and working*
*for the possibility of a better world.*

*For Caroline, who taught me that*
*faith should be interesting.*
*−Claire Brown*

*For my late grandfather, John McRay—*
*who finally left his long Advent of dementia*
*to dissolve at last into the Light.*
*−Michael T. McRay*

# Contents

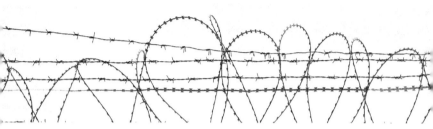

# Introduction

For many of us, Advent, the season that precedes Christmas, is marked by holiday parties, shopping and preparation, and end-of-the-year business. But in the Christian liturgical tradition, this season is one of penitence and preparation. Before the joy of Jesus' birth at Christmas, we walk through weeks of uncertainty about the world, repentance for our sins, and grappling with our need for God's intervention and God's call to us to address the injustices of the world. We prepare our hearts for God's coming through faithful work and prayer. We keep our hand to the plow while we search the skies for signs of God's presence. In the lectionary Gospel readings appointed for each year, the first Sunday of Advent is greeted with the news that the world is terribly broken. Fear and oppression and need are rampant. In our age and every age, it seems that our world needs God's peace more than ever. "Be prepared," encourages Matthew 24:36-44. "Stay alert!" says Mark 13:24-37. And when you see war, strife, and need, writes Luke in chapter 21, verses 25-36, "You know that God's kingdom is near." In those moments when life and the world are in the most turmoil, that is when we must keep watch for God's surprising presence. That moment of hopelessness or need or fear is the moment when holy grace and justice make themselves known.

The dream of this Advent reader came after a year of social and political upheaval around the world. Michael and I had spent the evening facilitating a story-sharing process with college students, watching their empathy and social awareness blossom in the span of a few hours. Afterward, reflecting on the experience, we talked about the spiritual resources folks need to prompt and sustain social action. How can we put into practice greater awareness for others, actively resist systems of social oppression and harm, and nourish our faith along the way? Where have we received the encouragement, support, conviction, and epiphanies that sustain our work? How can Christians, in particular, take seriously the command of God to love our neighbors as ourselves? How can we accept Christ's invitation to keep active watch, seeking God and doing the work of justice and peace?

Our hope is that *Keep Watch with Me* offers one way. The season of Advent offers us the opportunity to pause in our busy work and lives, to take stock of who and where we are, to repent, and to seek out the voice and movement of God's Spirit in the world, one another, and ourselves. This collaborative daily reader has stories, prayers, practice, and wisdom to help us do just that. It is written by peacemakers for peacemakers. Our contributors are an incredible line-up of folks from around the world: black, white, LGBTQ+, Latinx, Palestinian, incarcerated, indigenous, Australian, American,

Irish, South African, clergy, laity, activists, authors, organizers. Their insights, reflections, and prayers are full of vision and gritty hope to sustain us in the daily call to be makers of peace and keep watch for God's presence and work around us.

Each day's reading is accompanied by a spiritual practice that I have composed. When we offer spiritual practices in this Advent reader, we are talking about small experiments in praying, writing, acting, imagining, and relating to others that might help us connect with God in our daily lives. The daily practices accompanying each reflection are designed to give suggestions for integrating the reflections in your life and push you to think creatively about the "so what" of the *Keep Watch with Me* journey. Prayer and spirituality are not one-size-fits-all. If a practice feels too uncomfortable or simply doesn't resonate for you, feel free to let it go, revisit a different day's practice, create your own small ritual, or simply have a quiet moment with your reading. These practices are offered with confidence in the presence of God's spirit and openness to the myriad ways that God loves and leads us to peace.

Wherever you are in the journey of faith and work of peace-making, may this Advent season and *Keep Watch with Me* be a space of challenge, nourishment, and wonder. May you be encouraged as you keep watch for God's coming and presence in the world about you and strengthened to do the work of preparing and welcoming God with us.

*Claire Brown*
*January 2019*
*Chattanooga, Tennessee*

# DECEMBER 1

Michael T. McRay

# Text for the Day

*Therefore keep watch, because you do not know on
what day your Lord will come.*

*Matthew 24:42 (NIV)*

# Reflection

When I worked with Christian Peacemaker Teams in Hebron, the largest Palestinian city in the West Bank, one of our primary responsibilities was being present for confrontations between Israeli soldiers and Palestinian civilians. We needed to film and document all acts of aggression, hoping the scrutiny of international eyes might deter violence.

We needed to keep watch.

For those of us in the United States, the last few years have particularly highlighted the deep divisions scarring our country. Many of us yearn for a better world, and we wonder how long we can wait.

Advent is all about waiting. It is about patience, expectation, and longing. We wait in hope for the arrival of something better than what we have now. This is a joyful hope.

But Advent is about ache too, because longing and waiting are also painful experiences. For our exiled friends in prison longing for freedom, for our oppressed brothers and sisters waiting for justice, for our loved ones on the streets dreaming of a warm home, waiting is agony.

Both Advent and peacemaking are experiences of hope, and hope is the stuff of survival. It's little wonder people who live in places of suffering are often filled with great hope and joy. As one Palestinian friend said to me, "What choice do we have but to hope? The alternative is death." We hope that something more beautiful is coming because we must, because the alternative is unbearable. This work of hope is a muscular work, filled with sorrow, faith, perseverance, and resilience.

In my study, teaching, and practice of peace building, I've learned that the work of peace is the work of preparation. We wait, yes, but we have much to do while we wait. My best friend, Jeannie Alexander, is waiting for her beloved to be freed from the cage of prison. Year after year, she waits. But part of her waiting is working to make better laws so he can return home sooner. The waiting of Advent, like the waiting of peacemaking, is an active waiting. As the African proverb says, "When you pray, move your feet."

We watch, we wait, we work.

Part of the truth of our world is that it is broken and breaking more every day. But that is only part of the truth. Our world is also a place of beauty, love, and unfathomable generosity. There is kindness; there is laughter; there is healing. In a conversation with Bill Moyers, Thomas Cahill once said, "I have come to the conclusion that there are really only two movements in the world: one is kindness and the other is cruelty."[1]

I want to be part of the movement toward kindness, one where we might begin speaking to and about one another with something like love. I do believe that a kinder world is on the way. I believe it because I must, and I will watch for it, with eyes open and feet moving.

Will you keep watch with me?

# Prayer

*Jesus of the vigil,*
*you told us to keep watch,*
*to stay alert for what is coming.*
*Bless us with the strength*
*to watch,*
*to wait, and*
*to work*
*this Advent season,*
*so that your kingdom which is here*
*and is still to come*
*may be realized in its fullness.*
*Because if we do not keep watch,*
*we may miss it.*
*Amen.*

# Practice

As you begin this Advent journey, take a moment and consider what has drawn you to greater intentionality in this season. What questions and concerns burden you? What hopes draw you? What are you called to keep watch over in yourself and the world? Write or sketch some thoughts, setting your intention for this inner work of keeping watch with and for God among us this Advent. Keep this reflection as a reminder through the coming weeks.

# Bio

Michael T. McRay is a writer, facilitator, and story-practitioner living in Nashville, Tennessee. He's the author of multiple books, including the forthcoming *I Am Not Your Enemy: Stories to Transform a Divided World* (Herald Press, 2020). Michael is the Southeast regional manager for the global story nonprofit Narrative 4, and he also hosts Tenx9 Nashville Storytelling. He holds a graduate degree in conflict resolution and reconciliation from Trinity College Dublin at Belfast. He leads narrative retreats and speaks on story, conflict, reconciliation, and forgiveness. You can follow him @michaeltmcray on social media and through his blog at www.michaelmcray.com.

---

1. For the video of this interview, see http://billmoyers.com/segment/thomas -cahill-on-the-peoples-pope/.

# DECEMBER 2

Claire Brown

## Text for the Day

*Restore us, God!*
    *Make your face shine so that we can be saved!*

*Lord God of heavenly forces,*
    *how long will you fume against your people's*
    *prayer?*

                            *Psalm 80:3-4*

# Reflection

As a mom, I'm actively engaged in the nonprofessional peace-making of raising a toddler. Our child has unbounded curiosity and unbounded feelings. Massive dramas of disappointment, frustration, failure, and grief play out each day, and I must practice presence and compassion. Sitting with those big toddler feelings has been shown to better develop resilience, empathy, peace and calm in children over the long haul.

Practicing this with my child takes time, slows me down. It reminds me to practice it with myself. I feel disappointment, frustration, failure, and grief: with national politics and inequitable development, with the church's anxious idolatry of institution, with my own inner struggles as the days shorten and demands of writing, ministry, and parenthood feel endless, with the backdrop of our 24-hour news cycle of suffering.

Psalm 80 is the prayer of a suffering people who look at their lives and see only God's absence: How long will you be angry? Restore us! They are abandoned, shamed, alone, hopeless. They are carrying more than anyone can bear.

But we know that the tantrum, the prayer of a moment, a song of emotion, are never the whole picture.

Year after year, we go through the season of Advent, a liturgical season of penitence and preparation, as we anticipate Christmas, the celebration that God always intervenes. We sit with the already and not-yet of Jesus' coming. We read lamentations and prophecies of judgment with knowledge of peace. For Christians, silence, waiting, and death are not the end of the story, but we must sit with them.

Our sorrows are here and now. Our worries are life and death for ourselves and for the people we love. They need holy attention. And they are not the whole picture.

This Advent, we keep watch together so that we might grow a gritty, holy hope. We encourage one another to active peace building. We are choosing to do the hard inner work of being still, grieving, hoping, noticing, and becoming a little more peaceful within so that, as the apostle writes, we would be strengthened and faithful, in fellowship with Christ's work of peace incarnate (1 Corinthians 1:9).

# Prayer

*Christ, you who went up to the mountains to go deep within yourself, who always returned to the places of the people, who needed others to keep watch with you—may we find comfort in your humanity, in knowing that you have felt all this too. Give us the strength to be present to this moment, and the vision to see your holy and whole picture. Amen.*

# Practice

Take a moment today to sit quietly and consider: What situations, feelings, relationships, or concerns fill up your heart and mind and masquerade as the whole picture? As you name and consider sometimes overwhelming realities, take a few deeper than normal breaths. Squeeze and release your fists or shoulders, letting go of the internal tension that builds in our bodies with suffering and stress.

# Bio

The Reverend Claire Brown is an Episcopal priest, writer, partner, and mama living in Chattanooga, Tennessee. Her work focuses on the connections between the Eucharist, transformative spiritual practice, and community ethics. Claire is a graduate of Vanderbilt Divinity School, the Shalem Institute for Spiritual Formation, and the School of Theology at Sewanee. She blogs at revclairebrown.com about parenthood, embodiment, theology, and the church.

# DECEMBER 3

## Whitney Kimball Coe

## Text for the Day

*The L*ORD *said, "Go out and stand at the mountain before the L*ORD. *The L*ORD *is passing by." A very strong wind tore through the mountains and broke apart the stones before the L*ORD. *But the L*ORD *wasn't in the wind. After the wind, there was an earthquake. But the L*ORD *wasn't in the earthquake. After the earthquake, there was a fire. But the L*ORD *wasn't in the fire. After the fire, there was a sound. Thin. Quiet.*

*1 Kings 19:11-12*

# Reflection

Every time Advent rolls around, small purple signs begin appearing at St. Paul's Episcopal Church in Athens, Tennessee, dispatching us to "Slow down. Be quiet. It's Advent."

Much like the Hanging of the Greens at the Baptist church next door, my parish transforms for the Advent season overnight.

All at once, the halls, classrooms, sanctuary, and even the bathroom stalls are awash in purple flyers reminding us to slow down, be quiet, and know Christ is coming into the world. You can meditate on that promise while washing your hands or robing in the choir room or making your way to the altar for the Eucharist.

Parishioners are encouraged to pick up a handful of purple missives, take them home and hang them in places where we're most likely to see them.

It's now a sort of joke that the people of St. Paul's wait for Christ in their bathrooms.

My purple sign is indeed hanging on my bathroom mirror. It's the first thing I see in the morning and the last thing I see at night.

"Slow down. Be quiet. It's Advent."

Over the years, this bathroom tradition has informed a practice of letting go—letting go of distractions, letting go of the weight of the world, and especially, letting go of anything that is not love.

As I brush my teeth, the words stare back at me, and I can't help but meditate on how to make room for Christ in my super-anxious, hyperaware, socially righteous, crusading life.

The call of Advent is to practice putting down our desperate, human need for approval and fall in love with Jesus all over again, and to remember that *nothing short of God's love claims us*. We are children of God, and that is enough.

The culture of the moment demands our allegiance to political parties, ideologies, and hashtag movements to save our lives. We are encouraged to be thought-leaders, innovators, producers; to build power, to organize, to be woke, to be the fire or put it out. Our world is heavy with tragedy and injustice that sear and break our hearts, and the work of overcoming evil sometimes overshadows the true call to be love in the world.

In the face of suffering, we too often surrender Christ's light to reactionary grief, anger, and Twitter, and we forget to ask, *What would Love have me do in this moment?*

Advent reminds us that the work of love is a practice, not a competitive sport. It's not a win-lose or a zero-sum game. For Christians, seeing Christ's light in another is a way of being in the world, a practice that manifests as peacemaking, relationship-making, and reconciliation with the people right in front of you.

"What would Love have me do in this moment?"

Advent arrives each year to mercifully help us indwell the burning truth that we are named and claimed by God and nothing else. So, slow down and know. Be quiet and know. Christ's light is in you and everyone else too.

That's plenty to meditate on while you brush your teeth.

# Prayer

*Lord of all light and love, help me see Christ in
every human being, no exceptions. Open my
heart to what you would have me do next in
Love's name. Be my guidepost when I wake in
the morning and when I lie down at night, and
help me, help me, help me, Lord, to slow down,
be quiet, and watch for Christ's light in the
world.*

# Practice

Today, participate with Whitney and her church by making
your own Advent sign. You can borrow the St. Paul's phrase, "Slow
down. Be quiet. It's Advent," or create your own from these and your
own reflections. Hang your sign where you will see it daily.

# Bio

Whitney Kimball Coe serves as coordinator of the National Rural Assembly, a movement geared toward building better policy and more opportunity across the country for rural communities. In 2017, she was a featured speaker at the inaugural summit of the Obama Foundation and a guest on the radio program *On Being* with Krista Tippett. In 2018, she spoke at the Aspen Ideas Festival. Her focus on building civic courage in communities is directly tied to a practice of participation in her hometown of Athens, Tennessee, where she lives with her husband, Matt, and daughters, Lucy and Susannah.

# December 4

Shantell Hinton

## Text for the Day

*As he was thinking about this, an angel from the Lord appeared to him in a dream and said, "Joseph son of David, don't be afraid to take Mary as your wife, because the child she carries was conceived by the Holy Spirit. She will give birth to a son, and you will call him Jesus, because he will save his people from their sins."*

*Matthew 1:20-21*

# Reflection

Never before has Jesus' conception given me more pause than it does in our current political climate. While I am humbled by my wholehearted belief in the birth of our savior, I am also hard pressed to make sense of the ways in which the faith communities of which I have been a part taught me to accept the conspicuous circumstances surrounding Mary's unplanned pregnancy.

I suppose the account in Luke makes the virginal conception more palatable, insofar as Mary reportedly responded favorably to the angel who brought her news of God's plans for her to bear the Messiah. However, I am still captured by how coldly Joseph initially responded to Mary's situation. Though the text records that Joseph was a righteous man and wanted to dismiss Mary privately, it also suggests that Mary would face public disgrace. I can't help but wonder if Joseph also desired to distance himself from such scrutiny.

While pregnancy beyond the confines of marriage continues to carry a stigma in our context, it seems a righteous task to think more broadly about how sexual shame was at play in Joseph's decision to leave Mary. Perhaps it is idealistic of me to imagine a world in which Joseph would never have had to question Mary's account of what had happened to her, of why she had become pregnant beyond her control. But still, I wonder. Would Joseph have claimed the illegitimate son if the angel never showed up?

In the past years as the United States watched the rise of the #MeToo movement and the public hearing of Dr. Christine Blasey Ford and Judge Brett Kavanaugh, our culture has had many weighty conversations around sexual consent. In the aftermath, I asked myself, what would it take for our culture to find women's claims to be truthful and legitimate? How are we allowing societal norms to shame us into abandoning the gifts of God to which we have been called? Where are we too righteous, as Joseph was initially, to find mercy for any #MeToo? How do we believe and listen to those who have been impregnated with the stories that still live within their bodies? Must women carry Messiahs in their wombs before we see or value them as women, worthy of honor, *regardless*?

I can't speak to what will come of the myriad issues we face concerning women's reproductive rights and safety. Yet having lived through my own sexual shame and trauma, I can say that I see God's hand at work again in this Advent season. God's hand is beckoning us to question the ways we allow people to live in, stand in, and share their truths. And it is my prayer that we will be willing to see the testimonies of women like Dr. Blasey Ford, Tarana Burke, and Anita Hill. They are certainly clarion angels of the Divine, as holy gifts pointing us toward God's desire that we believe women—for their names are Emmanuel, "God with us."

# Prayer

*God, give us ears to hear your messengers, the women you have entrusted with your truth and presence. May we uncover shame and prize the dignity of every person. Amen.*

*Claire Brown*

# Practice

Today, holding in mind Shantell's reflection about shame and honor, open a Bible and slowly read the first chapter of Matthew. Invite God to be with you in this reading. Read the chapter a second time. See what images stand out to you, or where your imagination connects you into the story.

# Bio

The Reverend Shantell Hinton, MDiv, currently serves as the assistant chaplain at Vanderbilt University and is a recent graduate of Vanderbilt Divinity School. Shantell received a bachelor of engineering degree from Vanderbilt University and an MS in electrical engineering from Colorado State University. She has worked as a process control engineer in private industry and a worship coordinator for her church. Her research/interests include the intersections of activism and public theology, pastoral care, creating liturgy, and freelance writing.

# December 5

Becca Stevens

## Text for the Day

*From ancient times,*
*no one has heard,*
*no ear has perceived,*
*no eye has seen any god but you*
*who acts on behalf of those who wait for him!*
                              *Isaiah 64:4*

# Reflection

Sometimes I feel scared to stop and wait. It seems counterintuitive. I have been trying to grow a movement for women's freedom for decades through the work of Thistle Farms while pastoring a church and raising kids. I am always pushing ahead to stay on top of bills, ahead of the curve, or in front of the current issues. Waiting feels like it ruins my day. It's like letting froth die on a fresh latte or watching a muse move on to a more alert host upon which to rest. The fear of waiting is ridiculous, but it is part of the fragile ground upon which I tread in my own anxiety.

Is it hard for you to wait? In your quest to seek justice or to finish a to-do list, is waiting the stress? I am pretty sure I have said or thought *Hurry up!* in every line I have ever been in, whether it's in a grocery store or airport customs or the never-ending Nashville traffic or even a Communion line at church. It rarely feels like the "first will be last." It sometimes feels like people ahead of me are playing on their phone or asking too many questions and not moving at the speed with which I believe efficiency is maintained. *Go*, I hear myself saying on tarmacs, in carpool lines, and as my children learned to tie their shoelaces.

This Advent, though, I am hearing myself say a different word for the first time. For the first time, I can hear the warning from Isaiah as he reminds all seekers of peace and justice to wait and listen.

Unless I am willing to wait, I will not perceive the author of all justice. Unless I am willing to slow down, my ears will miss the voice of peace. So, my word for the first time this Advent is *stop*. Stop everything and perceive God!

I know everything is moving so fast, and when I stop, I can finally see it flying by. My husband's parents both died this fall, we are ushering one of our children off to college, and Thistle Farms has outgrown me. If I—or you—don't stop, we will pass ourselves by.

I want to breathe and not move and simply wait. Wait with grace as the light stays red, as my children take forever packing, and as women come to the decision to leave the streets and live in the community of Thistle Farms.

So, I offer you the word *stop* with all love and hope for the best Advent of your life. I offer you that word in the spirit of Isaiah, who longs for all of us to be with God.

Stop and wait.

# Prayer

*God, grant me the grace and space to slow myself, to wait and notice, that my heart and my hands would be ready to receive what you are offering. Amen.*

*Claire Brown*

# Practice

Today, find a comfortable seat and rest your open palms on your lap. Take a few deeper than normal breaths to find quiet and grounding. What are you waiting for? Is it known or unknown? Large or small? How are you finding the waiting? Imagine this awaited something sitting in your open palms, resting, not grasped. Imagine it, behold it, sit still with it, and give love to the awaited thing. Give love to yourself in your waiting.

# Bio

The Reverend Becca Stevens is an author, speaker, priest, social entrepreneur, and founder and president of Thistle Farms. After experiencing the death of her father and subsequent child abuse when she was five, Becca longed to open a sanctuary for survivors offering a loving community. In 1997, five women who had experienced trafficking, violence, and addiction were welcomed home. Now more than twenty years later, Thistle Farms continues to welcome women with free residences that provide housing, medical care, therapy, and education for two years. Becca has been featured in the *New York Times*, on *ABC World News,* and NPR, and was named a 2016 CNN Hero and a White House "Champion of Change."

# DECEMBER 6

## Jacob Davis, #308056

## Text for the Day

*How long will you forget me, LORD? Forever?*
  *How long will you hide your face from me?*
*How long will I be left to my own wits,*
  *agony filling my heart? Daily?*
*How long will my enemy keep defeating me?*
*Look at me!*
  *Answer me, LORD my God!*
*Restore sight to my eyes!*
  *Otherwise, I'll sleep the sleep of death,*
    *And my enemy will say, "I won!"*
    *My foes will rejoice over my downfall.*
                                    *Psalm 13:1-4*

# Reflection

Those of us with impossible prison sentences are exiles, modern scapegoats in the most profound sense. We have sentences that do not allow for our bodily redemption outside of prison walls no matter the extent of our rehabilitation or deep desire for restoration. We are told to keep hope and to maintain a positive appearance for the rare free individual allowed to look upon us. But in truth, we who wait in exile have one task before us: to swim against a numbing tide that never seems to end. Each time we give up and give in to despair, each time we stop struggling against the tide and slide into selfish forgetfulness, it gets harder to remember why we chose to battle for our human dignity in the first place.

Who wants to live with constant tension? Who needs the pain, the ache, the lack of certainty, the discouragement of a vacant horizon? A thin possibility of hope echoing through our memory and an endless litany of self-accusation—are these alone supposed to sustain us? We are accustomed to hope coming to the point of our fingertips, a life raft just out of reach, only to be swept into the tides of political change again, leaving us adrift.

Still, even if we know we will fail, we should press on. We know it is easier to relax and drift, but we should remember what is at stake.

What is at stake?

When we struggle at the surface, we have at least a chance at clarity. Is it not the breathtaking canopy unfolding above us that inspired our commitment the first time we broke through? Yet in time, this endless expanse defines our true dilemma: not even the meaning of all this is guaranteed; and oh, how we struggle for meaning. What is the meaning of suffering when the only prescribed purpose is pain? Day in and day out, I see endless broken solutions being applied to broken people in a willfully flawed system. The moments of clarity are too brief. Still, I hear a whisper, *Keep holding on.*

And we can, if we can remember that even in exile God has not forgotten us—our names are etched upon God's heart. One day they could be etched upon the hearts of men and women again, so I hold on. I struggle. Each day of my life I wait in advent.

Would you choose this struggle even if you knew this torturous hope would yield no fruit? But what soul is worthy of revelation who never bore this burden?

# Prayer

*God of the thin places, of dying hope, God
of the waters of forgetfulness and waters of
remembrance, we remember.*

*Though we remember often only in echoes,
fragments of dreams, a half memory turning over
and over in our mind, still, we do remember.*

*We will chase the ghost of you, God, even after
we have lost all reason to believe in the substance.
Oh please, chase our ghost too.*

*In the beginning you moved upon our waters—
and we—we filled our lungs with you, willing to
drown in your ecstasy. And now the waters are
cold, and our voices echo off the endless expanse
between I and thou.*

*Can you feel our souls adrift in the poverty of our
longing? Have you fallen asleep, God, while we
were keeping watch? Awake, Beloved, or if you
must rest, rest in our bones and wrap yourself in
our weary souls. We need to come home, but for
now we wait, adrift in your sleep, waiting for the
dream. And that is enough for now.*

*Amen.*

*Jeannie Alexander*

## Practice

Share in Jacob's question: What is at stake?

In your daily life, relationships, and work, what is at stake? In your faith and waiting, what is at stake? For you? For your community? Sit with this question for several deeper-than-usual breaths. Today, if the answer to that question is overwhelming, speak it out loud to God, letting the answer be released from you and given to the Listener and Comforter who is the true Peacemaker. If today the answer to that question gives grounding and determination, write it down on a note card and carry it into your day as a reminder and motivation for your work of peacemaking.

## Bio

Jacob Davis is a writer and a student who has lived in the Tennessee prison system since 1998, where he is serving a life sentence with possibility of parole, which in Tennessee is fifty-one years. He is a founding member of No Exceptions Prison Collective and the interfaith community Harriet Tubman House. His work has been published in *Contemporary Justice Review, Huffington Post, Leaven*, Tenx9 Nashville Storytelling, and *Scalawag*. He is the beloved partner of Jeannie Alexander (December 23), and a devoted son, brother, and uncle.

# December 7

Jarrod McKenna

## Text for the Day

*So then, from this point on we won't recognize
people by human standards. Even though we used to
know Christ by human standards, that isn't how we
know him now. So then, if anyone is in Christ, that
person is part of the new creation. The old things
have gone away, and look, new things have arrived!*

*All of these new things are from God, who reconciled
us to himself through Christ and who gave us the
ministry of reconciliation.*

*2 Corinthians 5:16-18*

# Reflection

Real hope is hard.

I confess how hard I find it to open daily to my own pain, let alone hold my heart open for a hope that's wide enough to envelop Aleppo, Haiti, Don Dale, Manus, Baghdad, Hebron, the Great Barrier Reef. Or even just enough hope for reconciliation with those from whom I am estranged this Christmas.

Often the only hope we have is that others won't peer behind the thin positivity or religiosity in which we wrap our protective indifference and dysfunction. We scramble to shield our souls against being pierced by the hope of a Savior who liberates through suffering-love, even to the point of a cross.

Sometimes hope must be sung. Trust and trembling are heard in song. Abraham Joshua Heschel remarked, "Music leads us to the threshold of repentance, of unbearable realization of our own vanity and frailty and of the terrible relevance of God."[1]

The unbearable relevance of hope is a hard song to sing. I have sung it in joy after news of friends getting married. I have sung it in despairing disbelief after news of a close friend being murdered. I have sung it knowing the goodness of community. I have sung it alone, to fight back the night, when I am worn out by sorrow.

Advent is about real hope, real holiness. Waiting in sober silence. In such silence, I have learned that real hope is hard. I am haunted in Advent with the holiness of hard-fought-for hope. Hope that is a fragile gift. Hope that daily requires the wrestling open of our hands and hearts to be received. The hope that demands a willingness to feel through the numbness. A willingness to hurt.

This kind of hope has nothing to do with silly—even if sincere—self-obsessed, religious control-games where we seek to manipulate God with our "morality" by "getting it right." True "righteous and devout" witness is far more terrifying: not moral achievements but sheer grace. The grace of control relinquished. The grace of brokenness embraced. The grace of forgiveness received and given. The grace and integrity of hope hung on to, through hell, for the long haul. That's the witness of Advent waiting.

Waiting for what? *When God's world will be made right.* Active waiting where we learn to say no to counterfeit consolation: simple answers, quick fixes and easy-outs that would protect us from entering in on the heartbreaking ache of God and the promised Messiah. In this season, may we have ears to hear. May our voices shake in awe of a God who saves by suffering love.

Real hope is hard. It calls from us a holiness which is not our own. May hope pierce our souls with Christ's victorious suffering-love that we, too, might lift our voice in song.[2]

# Prayer

*God, forgive me when I seek control and "right-*
*ness" and choose the path of fear that yields*
*violence. Strengthen me to partake in your*
*hope. Pry my hands loose from the grasping*
*and striving, and teach me to sing your wonder.*
*Amen.*

*Claire Brown*

# Practice

Most of us have our own litany of fears and sorrows that make it difficult to open our heart wide enough for hope. Set a timer for three minutes and write down anything that is preoccupying, sorrowful, painful, distracting, or anxiety-making. Freewrite the list until your timer goes off. Then fold the paper, and holding it in open hands, invite God's presence and care for all the things written there, perhaps repeating the prayer included above.

# Bio

Jarrod McKenna has been described by Civil Rights icon Rev. James Lawson as "an expert in nonviolent social change." McKenna is the Founding Director of CommonGrace.org.au, the Teaching Pastor at Sanctuary Church, Perth, Australia, and has spent the last 15 years sharing his home with asylum seekers, refugees, and others needing hospitality.

---

1. Abraham Joshua Heschel, *The Insecurity of Freedom: Essays on Human Existence* (New York: Farrar, Straus and Giroux, 1967), 246.

2. Adapted with author's permission from "The Fragile Gift of Hope" on ABC's Religion and Ethics website at abc.net.au.

# DECEMBER 8

Mark Charles

## Text for the Day

*All of us have become like one who is unclean,*
*and all our righteous acts are like filthy rags;*
*we all shrivel up like a leaf,*
*and like the wind our sins sweep us away.*
*No one calls on your name*
*or strives to lay hold of you;*
*for you have hidden your face from us*
*and have given us over to our sins....*

*Do not be angry beyond measure, LORD;*
*do not remember our sins forever.*

Isaiah 64:6-7, 9 (NIV)

# Reflection

Advent is the season of hope, the season of waiting for the coming of Christ. As Christians, we believe that our hope is found in Christ, and that the church, the Bride of Christ, is God's chosen instrument of revelation. But how do you offer hope when the church itself is the oppressor? When the church has committed countless violations in the name of Jesus?

In 2016, I had the honor of visiting an Anishinaabe (Ojibwe) elder and dear friend.[1] He was a Vietnam veteran, an accomplished writer, and a boarding school survivor. Boarding schools were a forced assimilation tactic employed by the US government and churches in their ongoing efforts to "kill the Indian to save the man." My friend had been diagnosed with cancer and had only a few months to live. He and his wife decided that his limited days would be spent cherishing every moment and relationship. After a long journey, I arrived at his house to spend a few hours with him. In his weakened state, he did not have the energy for prolonged visits, and I spent most of our time together sitting on his porch, listening to his stories.

Over our years of friendship, I had heard a trickle of his stories, but that afternoon the dam broke, and stories came flooding out. They were gut wrenching. Stories about how he was "converted" to Christianity in the boarding school, not because he liked Jesus but because he learned that students who said "the prayer" were given bigger portions at dinner. Stories about how the school used cigarettes to manipulate the behavior of the young Native students.

Stories about the suicide attempts of family members, the strict punishments by the boarding school administrators, and, worst of all, the sex education he received in the form of statutory rape by one of his teachers at this church-run boarding school.

I had heard stories like his before from second- and thirdhand sources. I had read stories like his before, of people I did not know. But that afternoon, the firsthand stories of my friend shook me. He was not angry, nor was he bitter. But he was honest. Brutally honest. And there were no words. There was nothing I could say. He was trying to make peace with his past and was deeply wrestling with his pending death. And there was nothing I could say. He knew I was a Christian, but he was not looking for Christ. Nor did I know how to offer Christ. So, we sat there. I listened. I hugged him. And we said our good-byes. He died a few months later.

How do you offer hope when the church itself is the oppressor? When the church has committed unspeakable violations in the name of Jesus?

I don't know, but I believe it begins with lament. And this Advent Season I pray the church will join me.

## Prayer

*[At the author's request, there is no written
prayer today. Only silence and lament.]*

## Practice

For people of faith and goodwill, hearing stories like that of
Mark's friend may prompt us to action and fixing. The discomfort
of our inherited wrongs makes us seek a solution, to jump ahead to
offering Christ without knowing how. The first spiritual practice we
are called to is grief. Reread the Scripture and the author's reflection.
Notice what feelings arise in you. Sit and breathe with those feelings
and observations, and offer them to God.

# Bio

Mark Charles is a dynamic and thought-provoking public speaker, writer, and consultant. He writes for Native News Online and his personal blog "Reflections from the Hogan." He served on the boards of the CCDA and the Christian Reformed Church of North America. Mark also consults with the Calvin Institute of Christian Worship and is a founding partner of a national conference for Native students called Would Jesus Eat Frybread?

---

1. The Ojibwe is a North American indigenous tribe within the larger group of Anishinaabe peoples.

# DECEMBER 9

Brian Ammons

## Text for the Day

*From the fig tree learn its lesson: as soon as its branch becomes tender and puts out its leaves, you know that summer is near. So also, when you see these things taking place, you know that he is near, at the very gates.*

*Mark 13:28-29 (ESV)*

# Reflection

I'm not much for raking leaves. I'm not much for yard work at all, to be honest, which is why we live in the woods. I do, however, love watching the leaves fall, and as I look out my window I notice they've gathered in their annual heaps and mounds on the deck. I notice, too, that I can now see the mountains I always know are there on the horizon, hidden until the leaves come down.

Now that winter is here, the leaves have done their falling. And though I know there's an official first day of the season that hasn't arrived yet, the cold has come. It's time for building fires to warm our living room and cuddling under wool blankets—and for me, that means winter. Winter, like summer, never seems to mark itself with a singular entrance. In these southern Appalachian Mountains that I call home, the dance between the changing seasons seems a bit chaotic, and the thermostat gets a workout with all its up and down rhythms. Then one day it's just here. The new season has come. It's winter, and in winter we take shelter—and we see more clearly.

I admit that I love the beginning of winter, though by February I'm tired of it and starting to long for the buds that emerge in March. I know that the up and down, clear and cloudy patterns will begin again, and there will be signs that summer is coming. But like winter, it won't be in an instant—just one day I'll notice, "Oh, it's here."

Perhaps this is the way of the commonwealth of God—the better world we are called to cocreate. Perhaps in these wintry seasons we are invited to take shelter and see more clearly so that as we enter into the chaotic growth of spring we may be better prepared to notice the summer as it comes. Seasonal metaphors seem strange for the kingdom, because their most distinct attribute is that they are temporary, changing . . . *seasonal.*

We are called to embody the kingdom in the here and now rather than in some far-off clouded paradise. Perhaps our noticing of God's ever-presence is more seasonal. Perhaps our need for a clear moment of arrival is ours—our longing for perpetual summer an attachment to a vision more ours than God's. Every peace-building justice worker I know recognizes that we are in a particularly tough season—we are taking shelter when we can, going out to tend to those left exposed, and looking through bare trees toward a distant horizon. This is not our first winter, and it will not be our last. It would be arrogant and disrespectful of the resilient teachers that came before us to think otherwise.

So in this Advent, this season of lengthening nights, we light a candle with expectant hope and clarity to witness the in-breaking of God. New leaves will grow, perhaps even before I've gotten around to sweeping this year's from my deck.

## Prayer

*God of the changing seasons, in the cold of
winter, as we sit in hope and anticipation for
new life, grant us clarity and vision. When the
nights are long and the world seems dark, may
we remember the coming summer. Amen.*

## Practice

Brian's winter reflection gives a beautiful picture of the natural cycle of death and resurrection, whether a relationship, project, attitude, habit, job, or season of life. Imagine, write, or share with a friend something that seems bleak, sparse, or dying in this Advent season. Imagine, write, or share something that is budding or something that you hope will bloom soon.

# Bio

The Reverend Brian Ammons is the chaplain and director of spiritual life at Warren Wilson College, near Asheville, North Carolina. His work focuses on interfaith dialogue, vocational discernment, and disrupting the artificial divide between the pastoral and prophetic in a world of increasing "nones." He is an ordained Baptist minister and has taught, written, and spoken on the intersection of spirituality and sexuality—particularly around rethinking the conversations including LGBTQ+ people in the church. Brian also works alongside his husband, Gareth Higgins, leading retreats and planning festivals.

# DECEMBER 10

## Pádraig Ó Tuama

# Text for the Day

*The beginning of the good news about Jesus Christ, God's Son, happened just as it was written about in the prophecy of Isaiah:*

> Look, I am sending my messenger
> before you.
> He will prepare your way,
> a voice shouting in the wilderness:
> > "Prepare the way for the Lord;
> > make his paths straight."

*John the Baptist was in the wilderness calling for people to be baptized to show that they were changing their hearts and lives and wanted God to forgive their sins. Everyone in Judea and all the people of Jerusalem went out to the Jordan River and were being baptized by John as they confessed their sins. John wore clothes made of camel's hair, with a leather belt around his waist. He ate locusts and wild honey. He announced, "One stronger than I am is coming after me. I'm not even worthy to bend over and loosen the strap of his sandals. I baptize you with water, but he will baptize you with the Holy Spirit."*

*Mark 1:1-8*

# Reflection

Today, in 1830, Emily Dickinson was born. She wrote that her life was like a loaded gun. She wondered if you grew by melody or witchcraft. She spoke of hope being a thing with feathers. And she knew two kinds of loneliness. Her focus on her art is like a blade, or a lightning bolt.

She wrote fine letters, plenty of them, so if letters are a measure of love, then she loved a lot. She certainly loved her sister-in-law, her Irish maid, her big dog.

She spent a lot of time alone.

Her poetry is baffling and brilliant. With words and dashes, with rhymes and half-rhymes, she defined a poetic school that is, at times, like music, at other times like a punch. I avoided the recent film, not because Cynthia Nixon isn't brilliant, but because I couldn't imagine imagining Emily on something as straightforward as a screen. Her work goes beyond dimensions: in its incomprehensibility, in its incision, in its deathtongue, and in its love of bees and purple.

She didn't leave the townland of Amherst often. She didn't need to—she had hell and heaven enough:

> *The soul has moments of Escape —*
> *When bursting all the doors —*
> *She dances like a Bomb, abroad,*
> *And swings upon the Hours.*[1]

Dickinson shows us what is uncontainable in us—those wild worlds. In games about fantasy dinner guests, I always wonder if

I'd have the courage to summon her up. What would she eat? What would she say? Where would she come from, she who even God wouldn't tame?

It takes courage to live a life with integrity. With Emily Dickinson's birthday in mind, I read Mark's Gospel today. Mark is no fan of ease. And when Mark writes John the Baptist in his desert landscape, I find myself praising the uncontainable characters of the world, those wild ones who have always had the courage to say what they need to say. They feast on strange things, they gather unexpected people around them: people who do not understand what they are hearing, but know they need to listen.

And so John is in a wild place and people are coming to him. People from the countryside and the city come to hear this man with a blade for a tongue and eyes like fire, the man who eats things that sting and dresses in skins. He liked bees, too, or at least their honey. His eyes see the sky split open, and he is searching for a person who can hold power in one hand and peace in the other. He isn't interested in self-promotion, only in apocalypse: the carpet lifted, hidden things being shown.

Would I invite John to dinner? God, no. What would he say, sitting at my table in his skins, licking honey from my knives.

But I need John and his sharp tongue.

And I need Emily and all her heavens and hells.

Their wild words help me survive a wild world.

## Prayer

*In the name of the Bee*
*and of the Butterfly*
*and of the Breeze.*
*In the name of locusts*
*and wild words*
*and wild honey.*
*In the name of bombs*
*and breathing*
*and brilliance.*
*In the name of escape,*
*and engagement*
*and armour.*
*In the name of everything*
*and nothing*
*and whatever will save us.*
*In the name of this small moment.*
*Yes, this small moment.*
*This very small moment.*
*Amen.*

# Practice

Both Emily Dickinson and John the Baptist are people with sharp words. Their loyalty was to telling the truth, rather than making people feel comfortable. This is vital for our lives, but not always easy. Find a quiet moment and a physically comfortable seat, and place one hand on your belly. Place the other hand over your heart, and feel grounded and secured in your body. After a few deep breaths, consider an experience you've had with wild, sharp, truthful words. How did these words strike you? What is their invitation? You can return to this physical posture for grounding and security throughout your day, or any moment when you face a sharp word.

# Bio

Pádraig Ó Tuama is a poet and a theologian from Ireland. With interests in religion, conflict, and storytelling, he writes poetry that prowls around these concerns of the human heart. He teaches, writes, and leads retreats at home and abroad, as well as being a regular guest on radio, including *On Being with Krista Tippett*. From 2014 to 2019, he was the leader of the Corrymeela Community, Ireland's oldest peace and reconciliation organization.

---

1. Emily Dickinson, *The Poems of Emily Dickinson*, ed. R. W. Franklin (Cambridge: Belknap Press of Harvard University Press, 1999), 163.

# December 11

## Nontombi Naomi Tutu

## Text for the Day

*Comfort, comfort my people!*
*says your God.*
*Speak compassionately to Jerusalem,*
*and proclaim to her that her compulsory*
*service has ended,*
*that her penalty has been paid,*
*that she has received from the LORD's hand*
*double for all her sins!*

*Isaiah 40:1-2*

# Reflection

As soon as I hear Isaiah 40:1-11, I am reminded that as we are waiting for the arrival of Emmanuel. God is always waiting for us. The God for whom we wait never ever gives up on God's people. We might give up on ourselves or take our present circumstance as the end of the story, but our God always holds a promise of healing, of wholeness, and of redemption.

Growing up as a black child in apartheid South Africa, the words "Comfort, comfort my people" felt as though they were being spoken directly to us, the oppressed and marginalized. It was a word from God that we were never out of God's thoughts or removed from God's love. At that point in my life, the closest I could come to an image of God was the women of our community, who loved all us children unconditionally. God offered, in these words, the comfort that these mothers and grandmothers gave to us each and every day, in the words of love, empowerment, and dignity they poured into us, in direct contradiction to the messages we received from the government and media. Oppression and fear have never been God's dream for the people of God. No matter how trying and bleak life may appear, our God promises that She is ready to welcome us into the circle of Her love.

Living in the United States over the past years, I have found myself experiencing the fear and anger that I knew so well in apartheid South Africa. Each day the news covers some new assault on our humanity. It seems there is no end to the racist, sexist, anti-immigrant, homophobic, and Islamophobic rhetoric that comes from political and religious leaders. Over and over I am tempted to give up, to believe that this is the human story.

Isaiah reminds me that what happens in the world is not simply a human story, but that our story is the story of God who stands ready to accept our every move back to Her. God wants nothing but for us to experience the fullness of God's love. God offers us opportunity after opportunity to make our hearts ready to receive God's love.

Advent for me has always been about looking at the valleys, the crookedness, and rough places not just in the outside world, but also in our own hearts. Where are the places where we have elevated ourselves into little gods, pushing God out of Her rightful place? Where are the places in our lives that we have exiled ourselves from God's Word? In what ways are we shutting out the voice calling us to repentance, calling us to turn our deepest desires to align with those of God for ourselves and the world?

We wait now, knowing that God, too, is waiting. Waiting for us to recognize the depth of God's love for us.

*Maranatha*—Come, Lord Jesus.

## Prayer

*God our comforter, make plain to us the ways
that we have pushed away your comfort and
failed to receive your love. Give us the strength to
face the work of each day and acknowledge your
love, provision, and hope for your people. Amen.*
Claire Brown

## Practice

God brings us comfort in people, in words, in small acts of mercy from our community and small goodnesses of life. Today, don't hesitate to seek out a small comfort: a phone call to a loved one, a bath or meal, a quiet moment—whatever it is that provides comfort for you. When you find this moment, receive it as God's own love for you and give thanks for the particular moment of God's kingdom in and with you.

# Bio

The challenges of growing up black and female in apartheid South Africa have been the foundation of Nontombi Naomi Tutu's life as an activist for human rights. Those experiences taught her that our whole human family loses when we accept situations of oppression and how teaching and preaching hate and division injure us all. Her path to ordination has been one of struggle and wrestling with what a call to the priesthood means in our very divided world. The Reverend Tutu serves as cathedral missioner for Racial and Economic Reconciliation and missioner for Kairos West at All Souls Cathedral in Asheville, North Carolina. She is the mother of Tebogo, Mungi, and Mpilo.

# December 12

## Tony D. Vick

## Text for the Day

*Happy are those who trust in the LORD,*
*      who rely on the LORD.*
*They will be like trees planted by the streams,*
*      whose roots reach down to the water.*
*They won't fear drought when it comes;*
*      their leaves will remain green.*
*They won't be stressed in the time of drought*
*      or fail to bear fruit.*

*                              Jeremiah 17:7-8*

# Reflection

Having something to look forward to is essential for the human soul. As Christians, we look forward to Christmas as a time to celebrate the birth of our Savior and to enjoy time spent making memories with loved ones. Just a little bit of hope for something positive can feed a person's emotional needs for a long time.

In prison, where I've been since 1996, the holidays are a depressing and lonely time. The penitential time of Advent punctuates the painful emotions associated with the sins that brought us here, the sins that separated us from our families and communities and, perhaps, even from God. Not surprisingly, the suicide rate in prison climbs drastically during the Christmas season. I've been one of the lucky ones, though. At each of the seven prisons where I've lived during my incarceration, God has revealed rays of hope, allowing me to see light through the brokenness and depression. Each ray of hope feels like God's hands are wrapping me in his love, showing me that I am loved even while serving two life sentences for murder. Humbling—undeserved—overwhelming.

I now look forward to things that once seemed insignificant because they bring me hope. Anticipating a new flavor of ramen noodle soup at the commissary or expecting a Christmas meal provided by a local church become those "somethings" that lift my spirits and help me hang on. These days, I'm finding even greater hope because of the diligent work of prison-reform advocates both inside and outside the razor wire.

Staying afloat in the river of remorse, regret, and sorrow that flow through this place is difficult. But most inmates will eventually realize their hope of being released from prison. They inevitably have to face all the unresolved issues that have been frozen in time during their incarceration.

For this reason, citizens in many states are realizing the importance of prisoners' spending more of their time preparing for release. Education, job training, rehabilitative programs, religious services, volunteers, mentors, and pen pals inside the walls provide insiders with impressions of humanity. These "somethings" allow them to be successful in their first steps of freedom and not bogged down with the chains of years of dehumanization that currently follow many outside the walls.

At my current prison, we're forming a community of insiders who want to live in peace. In this special unit, we dwell together without fear of gang violence or of getting stabbed on the way to the shower. In this community, we are not relying solely on the state to provide us hope. We are encouraging each other, teaching each other, loving each other, and living with each other in harmony. This change we want begins with us. Small steps, small things to look forward to, small rays of hope—they all allow us to simply hang on. Just hang on.

# Prayer

*Let me, oh Lord, find peace and hope*
*in the midst of violence*
*May I find courage in the face*
*of fear from the brutality of*
*my surroundings*
*Remind me to look into the eyes*
*of your children and not focus*
*on the hateful words from their mouths*
*Let me, oh Lord, be the change*
*that I seek.*

# Practice

Tony points to the small, ordinary, and profoundly impactful ways that grace makes itself known in the limited environment of prison, the small somethings to look forward to that provide a much bigger hope. Whatever your environment, routine, or vocation, take time throughout today to look for small graces that keep you afloat, and look for an opportunity to provide such a small grace to another.

# Bio

Tony D. Vick is the author of *Secrets from a Prison Cell: A Convict's Eyewitness Account of the Dehumanizing Drama of Life Behind Bars*, with Michael T. McRay. Tony entered prison in 1996 after living thirty-four years in the free world as a closeted gay man. He is currently serving two life sentences for murder. While in prison, Tony has worked as a GED teaching assistant, clerk, and prison newspaper editor. Between 2010 and 2014, Tony completed five semesters in Vanderbilt Divinity School's Inside-Out program. Tony's thoughts on forgiveness were included in Michael T. McRay's book *Where the River Bends: Considering Forgiveness in the Lives of Prisoners*.

# December 13

## Gareth Higgins

## Text for the Day

*Comfort, comfort my people!*
*says your God.*
*Isaiah 40:1*

# Reflection

Over a decade ago, I nearly had the Christmas from hell.

A loving relationship had ended suddenly, a week before the day when we're supposed to get together with family and exchange gifts. The natural sadness I felt about the relationship was made worse by the fact that everywhere I went people were singing about bells and laughter and happily ever after. On the day itself, I was so sad I couldn't bring myself to go to see family.

My friend Kyle had invited me to his house for a drink. My heart was heavy. When I arrived, Kyle saw that I needed time and space and warmth. So he lit the fire, and when I told him I hadn't eaten all day, he took from the fridge plastic tubs of leftover Chinese takeout. Half eaten cashew chicken, a glass of wine, a little music in the background, the heat of the fire, the comforting presence of a friend.

One of the things that makes this season difficult for some is the sense of imposed happiness—the fact that we're supposed to feel, or pretend to feel, something deliriously joyful. Imposing emotions on folk is troubling, not least because it doesn't work, but also because coercion is never a manifestation of love. The fact that we are asked to squeeze ourselves into a feeling space we may not want to inhabit is made the more troubling by another fact: everyone seems to be running around buying things we don't need in an effort at expressing love. It's no wonder Scrooge wanted the season banned.

The pressure to perform joy should be consigned to the dustbin. What's valuable about Advent may well be the simplest things: that as we prepare for Christmas we can find happiness in the faces of friends, in the lights we put up to announce the season, in mulled wine and tasty food, in sharing in the bounty of the earth and her people, and in our willingness to treat strangers with warmth. It can all belong: the desire for connection, the bittersweet memory of loved ones no longer here, gratitude for the protection we find in each other, even the concern for justice as we consider the suffering that has led to the production of the products we might have stressed ourselves out to buy.

Over a decade ago I began the worst Christmas of my life, but alongside leftover cashew chicken, in the presence of a friend, the truths of the season permeated me: that love is stronger than death, that we are called into communities of mutual service, that sometimes it is I who need to let go and allow someone to do the heavy lifting, and sometimes it is I who am called to do the carrying. That the season we mark in December—Advent—is a signifier of a year-round invitation to comfort each other.

# Prayer

*God of comfort,*
*sometimes life is full of pain.*
*Sometimes, it hurts like hell.*
*Sometimes, it's filled with*
*fear and loneliness.*
*May we be present for those*
*who are alone,*
*comfort those*
*who are hurting,*
*and find joy*
*in the simple things.*
*And please help us remember that in these times*
*of ache,*
*it's okay to ask for help—*
*because we need each other.*
*Amen.*

*Michael T. McRay*

## Practice

Gareth reminds us that the seasons of Advent and Christmas can be emotionally complicated. The spiritual practice today is simple: if you need someone to carry you, reach out. If you find yourself present, able, and full, consider who around you might need lifting today.

## Bio

Gareth Higgins grew up near Belfast, northern Ireland, and now lives in North Carolina. He writes and speaks about connection to the earth, cinema and the power of dreams, peace and making justice, and how to take life seriously without believing your own propaganda. He's happy to be a work in progress. If you'd like to connect with his work, have a look at www.garethhiggins.net, www.theporchmagazine.com, and www.newstoryfestival.com.

# DECEMBER 14

## Charles Strobel

## Text for the Day

*In days to come…*
*they shall beat their swords into plowshares,*
*and their spears into pruning hooks;*
*nation shall not lift up sword against nation,*
*neither shall they learn war any more.*
*Isaiah 2:1, 4 (NRSV)*

# Reflection

The Advent Season offers a beautiful vision for all those working for peace, reassuring us that the time we spend waiting and watching will have divine meaning, purpose, and resolution. For we are told that "in days to come" an overarching plan will unfold. We believe the plan itself is God's story of Divine Discontent.

The problem, of course, and the challenge, is to see our own lives as part of that divine story, and not just as a series of disconnected events.

What is this Divine Discontent? It is that feeling of dissatisfaction inside us whenever we yearn for a world without war, a nation without poverty, a city without homeless, a family without abuse, children without empty stomachs, and an economic system without greed. Overall, it is our hope for community in a world filled with loneliness.

We experience dissatisfaction because we know that we have not created the world that God imagines. We have not created the kingdom on earth as it is in heaven.

Yet we should be grateful that we are created this way. We should take heart that we can imagine a better life for everyone, a community in which all are welcomed. For when we do, perhaps without even knowing it, God's story of Divine Discontent becomes more and more our own.

So as we yearn more and more for the kingdom, we draw closer to it. Advent is the season of yearning. It heralds the breaking of the dawn. It is the promise of the Kingdom Come. "O come, O come Emmanuel." We await you.

# Prayer

*God of the unfolding story, draw us into friend-
ship with our Divine Discontent as a gift of your
Spirit. Give us the strength to keep longing for
your Kingdom Come, to keep returning to our
communities and our peacemaking in gratitude
for your guidance toward the world you imagine
for your creation. Amen.*

*Claire Brown*

# Practice

Today, take some time to consider, perhaps with journaling, the vision of your peacemaking work. What is the work of God's kingdom that calls you? Consider where that work is right now, the gap between the present moment and the holy imagination. Notice what feelings arise. Dissatisfaction? Gratitude? Longing? Sit with whatever comes, offering it back to God as your small part in the story of Divine Discontent.

# Bio

The Reverend Charles Strobel is a native of Nashville with degrees from St. Mary's College, Xavier University, and Catholic University. While serving as a parish priest, he welcomed homeless individuals into his church building for the night, which led to the creation of Room In The Inn in 1986. Nearly two hundred Middle Tennessee congregations now participate in the Room In The Inn Winter Shelter program, and as many as four hundred people are served daily at its downtown comprehensive center. He was instrumental in founding several other Nashville organizations that serve the homeless community and has served on numerous boards.

# December 15

Brittany Sky

# Text for the Day

*A voice is crying out:*
*"Clear the LORD's way in the desert!*
> *Make a level highway in the wilderness for*
> *our God!*
*Every valley will be raised up,*
> *and every mountain and hill will be flattened.*
> *Uneven ground will become level,*
> *and rough terrain a valley plain.*
*The LORD's glory will appear,*
> *and all humanity will see it together;*
> *the LORD's mouth has commanded it."*

*Isaiah 40:3-5*

# Reflection

On a cold December night we gathered in front of the Metropolitan Nashville Police Department with candles and banners and megaphones. I had never participated in a protest march before. But with the relentless news segments about yet another murdered unarmed black person, I knew I could no longer sit on my couch while others cried out for justice.

Leaders from the Nashville #BlackLivesMatter chapter talked to us about their experiences driving while black in Nashville. Others spoke about being wrongfully incarcerated and the years of life they lost behind bars. Another spoke of institutional injustices and prayed for better systems.

Still another spoke out for the black women who were victims of police brutality. And another talked about the cradle to prison pipeline and the extremely negative effects of stereotyping young black children as troublemakers. I stayed quiet, listening while my candle flickered.

Then, as we marched through downtown Nashville reciting civil rights chants, I reflected on what I learned from the speakers. It made me sick to think about young children being told they were bad, sent into hallways and excluded from opportunities to learn and grow. It made me heartbroken to know that many of the children would grow up believing they had no other option for their lives but to end up in prison. As a children's minister, someone called to teach and learn with kids, I was angry. No child should ever be taught to doubt an inherent worth as a child of God. My reciting turned to yelling, which turned into lamenting.

I believe an important part of waiting is lamenting the injustices all around us. These lamentations lead to actions. These actions lead to small in-breakings of God's kin-dom. When we call out, God makes a way.

That night as we marched through the city witnessing to our community and calling ourselves to better actions, I imagined what John the Baptizer must have felt preaching by the Jordan River. We called out for the admission of sin and proclaimed the healing that comes from asking for forgiveness. We called out, encouraging each person to look deep inside their hearts and to change the way our lives are lived—to take a full inventory of the ways we white folks are privileged and the ways we consciously or unconsciously oppress anyone who doesn't look like us. We called out for the chance at a full life, believing in more than violence and marginalization.

We are the not the one who is coming, but we have a responsibility to help prepare the way.

# Prayer

*God, we call out to you in the midst of our sin
and suffering. Surround us in your grace and love.
Open our eyes to the ways we are contributing to
the degradation of your holy children. Create in
us a clean heart, oh God. Help us to change the
ways we live our lives, unthinking and always on
autopilot. Make us aware of the pain and suffering
and move us to cry out. Move us to change. Help
us prepare the way for your kin-dom. Amen.*

# Practice

Today or this week, carve out time to consider where you might be called to grief and repentance, whether for a personal wrong or your participation in a social wrong. Grief and repentance are not easy or desirable, but Brittany reminds us of our complicated humanity, that even in our efforts to bring peace we cause harm or are complicit in systems of harm.

If they are helpful in your process, use these prayers of confession and absolution from the United Methodist tradition.

> *Merciful God,
> we confess that we have not loved you with our
> whole heart.
> We have failed to be an obedient church.
> We have not done your will,*

*we have broken your law,*
*we have rebelled against your love,*
*we have not loved our neighbors,*
*and we have not heard the cry of the needy.*
*Forgive us, we pray.*
*Free us for joyful obedience,*
*through Jesus Christ our Lord. Amen.*

*Hear the good news:*
*Christ died for us while we were yet sinners;*
*that proves God's love toward us.*
*In the name of Jesus Christ, you are forgiven!*[1]

## Bio

Brittany Sky is the senior editor of children's resources at The United Methodist Publishing House. Her vocation in life is to spread the love of God to all of God's children. She strives to provide every child with a safe, loving, inclusive, and open environment to grow and learn, through and with God. She holds an MA in Christian Education from Garrett-Evangelical Theological Seminary and an EMBA from Tennessee State University. In 2016, Brittany authored and edited the *Deep Blue Bible Storybook*, and in 2019, she authored and edited the *Bible Basics Storybook*. She ranks the loves of her life in the following order: her husband, Michael; her dogs, Charlie and Lily; and coffee.

---

1. "A Service of World and Table 1," *The United Methodist Hymnal* (Nashville, TN: The United Methodist Publishing House, 1989), 8.

# December 16

Tarek Abuata

## Text for the Day

*Let me hear what the LORD God says,*
  *because he speaks peace to his people and to his*
  *faithful ones.*
  *Don't let them return to foolish ways.*
*God's salvation is very close to those who honor him*
  *so that his glory can live in our land.*
*Faithful love and truth have met;*
  *righteousness and peace have kissed.*
*Truth springs up from the ground;*
  *righteousness gazes down from heaven.*
*Yes, the LORD gives what is good,*
  *and our land yields its produce.*
*Righteousness walks before God,*
  *making a road for his steps.*

*Psalm 85:8-13*

# Reflection

As a Palestinian raised in Bethlehem, my people and I have waited in hope for decades, and my heart and hand have done God's peace work for twenty years. Waiting for the comfort of Isaiah, the restoration of Psalm 85, and the baptism of the Spirit during Advent Season, many times I despair. I continue to ask God, "Oh Lord, when will this come to be? It has been decades. How much longer?"

Six-year-old children forced to go through checkpoints on their way to school, parents standing against the rubble opposing the demolition of their children's homes, and grandparents weeping under the cut-down hundred-year-old olive tree they raised and knew before their own children. These are the scenes of hopelessness that I've experienced on multiple occasions in working in Hebron, Palestine.

Isaiah preaches that it is in the wilderness that we prepare the way for the Lord, where we make straight in the desert a path for our God. Likewise, Mark preaches that it is a voice of one calling in the wilderness that asks us to prepare the way for the Lord and to make straight paths for him.

It is also in this wilderness where I called unto God for years to answer my peoples' call for justice. It is in this wilderness that we at Friends of Sabeel North America call upon the church to implement justice for the Palestinian plight. It is in our joint work that we call upon our governments to make straight in the desert a path and to prepare the way for the Lord. With wrenched hearts and faint voices we continue asking God: "Where is your justice, God? When will your path come to be?"

I now see that the Divine Silence is Advent, the time of cleansing, the time of preparing ourselves for what's to be, and what's to come. It is the time for us to do our internal spiritual work, and a time for us to use our despair to open our hearts to welcome the birth and baptism that will comfort us in love.

With this new birth of our spirits, the spiritual birth comes, as a child, vulnerable and strong. Baptized with the Spirit, the child works in our hearts to engender a spiritual alignment where God's paths are straightened and lit with spiritual light and intentions. This is not the end, but the beginning of the journey on God's path. From that place, we no longer question God's silence, but we walk questioning our human silence and its sinful nature.

I pray that God continues to rattle our souls into discomfort as we do His work. I pray that God continues to question our silence, instills hopefulness in our hearts, and I pray for His promise of restoration. I know that it is possible, and I know that our work together in trust will get us to that promised land.

# Prayer

*Oh God who sees and hears,*
*sometimes it feels like you don't.*
*Sometimes it feels like we are lone voices*
*crying out in the wilderness and no one,*
*including you,*
*can hear us.*
*We want to believe you are listening.*
*Help our unbelief.*
*Give us the patience we need to survive,*
*the passion we need to be*
*your hands and feet of justice and peace in the*
*world,*
*and the trust that even though*
*you may be silent,*
*you are never far away.*
*Without these,*
*we may wither in despair.*
*Amen.*

*Michael T. McRay*

# Practice

Is silence comfortable or uncomfortable for you? If silence is a friend and ally, enjoy its company today. If silence doesn't come naturally or comfortably for you, seek it out in a small way: a calm morning moment, on your commute in place of music or the news, during a meal, or in brief meditation. Notice what comes up in the quiet today. Consider how Spirit might be in the thoughts and feelings that arise, and how Spirit is also in the edges of stillness around your busy mind, speaking "peace."

# Bio

Born into a Palestinian Christian family in Bethlehem, Tarek Abuata moved to Texas during the first Palestinian Intifada when he was twelve. He is the executive director of Friends of Sabeel North America. Previously, Tarek worked with the Christian Peacemaker Teams in Hebron, Palestine, for eight years, and the Negotiations Support Unit of the Palestinian Authority for a year. Tarek holds a JD from the University of Texas Law School.

# December 17

## Justin Coleman

## Text for the Day

*The L*ORD *God's spirit is upon me,*
*    because the L*ORD *has anointed me.*
*He has sent me*
*        to bring good news to the poor,*
*        to bind up the brokenhearted,*
*        to proclaim release for captives,*
*            and liberation for prisoners,*
*        to proclaim the year of the L*ORD*'s favor*
*            and a day of vindication for our God,*
*        to comfort all who mourn,*
*        to provide for Zion's mourners,*
*        to give them a crown in place of ashes,*
*        oil of joy in place of mourning,*
*        a mantle of praise in place of discouragement.*
*                                        Isaiah 61:1-3*

# Reflection

Isaiah 61 has occupied an important place in my Christian imagination for many years. I came to faith during my middle school years while reading a chapter a night of the Bible. I remember encountering Isaiah 61:1-2 first in Luke's citing of these verses in the fourth chapter of his Gospel.

Jesus finds himself in a synagogue on the Sabbath day, as was his practice, and he opens a scroll of the book of Isaiah and begins to read, "The Spirit of the Lord is upon me..." I can remember the thrill of imagining Jesus reading Scripture in synagogue just as I'd seen Scripture read in church. I was captivated by the scene and by the words. Jesus was saying to those gathered, Here is what I'm here to do: to offer good news to the poor, release to the prisoners, sight to the blind, liberation for the oppressed, and to announce the year of Jubilee.

This is what Jesus was about, which then raised the question: What should I be about? What should my Christian community be about in the world? Any passage from the Hebrew Bible that is quoted in the New Testament often assumes that the hearer had some sense of the context around the quotation. My study of Luke 4 then took me back to Isaiah 61. From this familiar passage of Scripture, verse 4 about the renewal of the city is the one that I hear quoted most infrequently. It reads:

> *They will rebuild the ancient ruins;*
> *they will restore formerly deserted places;*

> *they will renew ruined cities,*
> *places deserted in generations past.*
>
> *Isaiah 61:4*

This is a verse about our call to be a part of the renewal—the salvation of the streets. We must remember, however, how this chapter started: "The Spirit of the Lord is upon me, because . . . " The salvation of the streets begins with God's work in the individual and community that God has commissioned to move into the streets where God is already active in the work of renewing. This passage, then, is about a renewed and saved person and renewed and saved streets. In many communities around our country and world, we see cities or parts of cities that lie in ruin and have been under-loved for generations past.

How is God calling you to love the streets? How is God calling you to love the spiritual or material poor, the prisoner, the blind, the oppressed, those living in the midst of great inequity, and those who mourn?

Speaking of love for our communities and those who live within them, Father Gregory Boyle writes in his book *Tattoos on the Heart: The Power of Boundless Compassion*: "Soon we imagine, with God, this circle of compassion. Then we imagine no one standing outside of that circle, moving ourselves closer to the margins so that the margins themselves will be erased."[1] It's not just that those in the streets are saved by our ministry to them, but we are all renewed by the difference that our love for one another and relationship forged on the journey creates. In this way, we learn that our salvation is not *for* the streets, our salvation is *in* the streets.

## Prayer

*Oh God, we thank you for the love that we
receive from you. We pray that our love would
move to the margins so that those whom our
love finds there may transform us and increase
in us the margin to love. Amen.*

## Practice

Look at your day and work ahead, the responsibilities or appointments or routine in the coming hours. What is one way that you give of yourself and work to offer peace, help, or salvation in the world? What is one way that this work and self-giving has provided peace, help, or salvation to you as you give? What is one way that you have found salvation in the streets?

# Bio

The Reverend Justin Coleman is the senior pastor of University United Methodist Church in Chapel Hill, North Carolina. He is a graduate of Southern Methodist University and Duke Divinity School. Pastor Coleman has also served as the chief ministry officer for The United Methodist Publishing House, as lead pastor of the Gethsemane Campus of St. Luke's United Methodist Church in Houston, Texas, at the SMU Wesley Foundation, and in other college and youth ministry settings.

---

1. Gregory L. Boyle, *Tattoos on the Heart: The Power of Boundless Compassion* (New York: Free Press, 2010), 191.

# DECEMBER 18

## Ashley McFaul-Erwin

## Text for the Day

*"God's kingdom belongs to people like these children.
I assure you that whoever doesn't welcome God's
kingdom like a child will never enter it."*

*Mark 10:14b–15*

# Reflection

Let me take you back to April 9, 1998, in Larne, on the eastern coast of (the) north(ern)(of) ireland.[1] Like many other Thursday evenings my family and I were sitting in our living room watching TV. April ninth was the day before the Good Friday Agreement would be signed in our wee country. We were waiting for news of an agreement between our politicians. Many of us were waiting for the pain to stop.

As we watched the news that night, I saw people who looked like me, young people. I was eleven years old at the time. The camera showed a group of children, all dressed in school uniforms, being led in song by Irish folk musician Tommy Sands. They were standing outside the building where the politicians were deliberating. I did notice the children, but it was the drums that caught my eye. There were two different kinds of drums being played on that stage: lambegs and bodhráns. Lambegs are large, loud drums that are primarily associated with the Protestant community. Bodhráns are small handheld drums that are primarily associated with the Catholic community. As an eleven-year-old I had already picked up that these drums were not supposed to go together. Yet, as the country waited to see what our future would hold, these drums played together, and as they played the voices of the children rang out over them singing . . .

> *"Carry On, Carry On, You can hear the people singing,*
>
> *Carry On, Carry On, 'Til peace will come again."*

In that time of waiting, those voices of my peers and the different drums playing together gave me hope. A smile emerged across my face. As I look back on that day, I believe that was a holy moment: a holy moment of waiting when the veil between heaven and earth was lifted ever so slightly; a moment where drums were not being used to battle one another, but came together to accompany this young, yet ancient, cry for peace.

Seamus Mallon, Deputy First Minister of Northern Ireland from 1998 to 2001, would later say about this day, "The singing of the children was a defining moment for those around the table. We knew we must leave no stone unturned to find a way forward. We had no right to hold back the future from those young voices."[2]

In this Advent season, as we wait, may we also leave no stone unturned on our journeys toward peace. Seamus is right, we have no right to hold back the future, to hold back peace, from anyone, young or old.

As we walk towards the celebration of the arrival of God in the flesh, may we look to the wee ones in our midst. What are the eleven-year-olds, five-year-olds, sixteen-year-olds in our world saying to us? What world are they calling us into? We cannot ignore the children. As we wait for the Christ Child, may we listen to our own children and let them lead us.

## Prayer

*Christ the teacher, Christ the listener, when*
*you were a child, the temple leaders listened to*
*you. And you told us we must be like children*
*to really understand what you taught. May we*
*slow down and pay attention to the children*
*around us and be open to what they have to*
*teach. May we embody their curiosity and*
*wonder, their play, their songs and friendships,*
*their ability to stop and rest when they are tired,*
*and their humility to be held by someone who*
*loves them when they fall. Amen.*

*Michael T. McRay*

## Practice

Do you have any children in your family or community of faith or neighborhood? Today, take time to have a conversation with a child, or start correspondence with a note or phone call, and really listen deeply to them. Ask about their lives, thoughts, or activities. Really listen to what they tell you.

# Bio

The Reverend Ashley McFaul-Erwin was born in (the) north(ern)(of) ireland[3] and lived the first twenty-four years of her life in her hometown, Larne. Ashley attended Ulster University and worked as a youth and community worker in Belfast's Sandy Row before relocating to the United States. Ashley is a lifelong Presbyterian and in order to pursue a call to ministry as an openly queer person, she moved to the United States and found a home in the Presbyterian Church (USA). In 2011, Ashley moved to Nashville to participate in the PC(USA)'s Young Adult Volunteer program and serve with a local nonprofit. Since then Ashley has volunteered with the Iona Community in Scotland, completed her MDiv. at Vanderbilt Divinity School, and worked with young people within Tennessee's Juvenile Justice system and with women who are in addiction treatment. Ashley is a Minister of Word and Sacrament in the PC(USA) and is currently serving as the Community Outreach Pastor at Setauket Presbyterian Church, Long Island. In her spare time Ashley enjoys taking walks with her wife, Erica, and their two dogs. She also loves to get home to Larne (and Belfast, "the best wee city in the world") as much as possible and is a self-confessed Irish rugby fanatic.

---

1. In the part of the world I call home, the name of the six counties on the northeastern part of the island is somewhat contentious. In recognition of this, in writing I am choosing to use the title of a Pádraig Ó Tuama poem, (the) north(ern)(of) ireland, to recognize this complexity.

2. Seamus Mallon, quoted in Tommy Sands, *The Snowman: A Journey in Irish Music* (Dublin: Lilliput, 2005), 257.

3. See note 1 above.

# December 19

## Lindsey Krinks

## Text for the Day

*The LORD God's spirit is upon me,*
*     because the LORD has anointed me.*
*He has sent me*
*     to bring good news to the poor,*
*     to bind up the brokenhearted,*
*     to proclaim release for captives,*
*          and liberation for prisoners,*
*     to proclaim the year of the LORD's favor*
*          and a day of vindication for our God,*
*     to comfort all who mourn,*
*     to provide for Zion's mourners,*
*     to give them a crown in place of ashes,*
*     oil of joy in place of mourning,*
*     a mantle of praise in place of discouragement.*
*Isaiah 61:1-4a*

# Reflection

There is a kind of waiting that rubs you raw. A kind of hunger that can't be filled by bread alone. "Justice is like the kingdom of God," writes George Eliot. "It is not without us as a fact, it is within us as a great yearning."[1]

In this season of Advent, this season of winter and waiting, those of us in the Northern Hemisphere are approaching the longest night of the year known as the Winter Solstice. Trees in the forest sense the shifting seasons and send their energy to their roots, their core. They know what it takes to weather the winds that race from the North. They know what it feels like to hope with every fiber of their being that the present darkness does not have the final say.

The prophet Isaiah, well acquainted with darkness, prophesies that all who mourn and are oppressed will be given beauty instead of ashes, the oil of joy instead of mourning, garments of praise instead of a spirit of despair. They will raise up the former devastations and repair the ruined cities, he says (Isaiah 61:3-4).

Every time I read Isaiah 61, it has a visceral effect on me. As a street chaplain, my days are filled with people who mourn and are cast out by our present order. To imagine my friends on the streets finding comfort, good news, and liberation . . . To imagine our cities rebuilt by the underdogs and creation restored . . . My heart swells with longing and I feel weak in the knees.

It is no secret that things are not as they should be. The earth groans. Our collective wounds fester. Our leaders fail us. Wealthy developers inherit the earth and displace the poor from the shining cities they've raised. The homeless Christ shivers on street corners of indifference and wastes away behind layers of barbed wire. When will the ruined cities be repaired? When will the oil of joy anoint our scattered bones?

Perhaps part of being alive, part of being *awake*, means being in touch with this deep sense of longing. We long for warmth, community, and love. We long for justice and restoration, for something—someone—to break through all this darkness and bring good news.

A couple years ago, a friend gave me a moonflower seedling for my garden. The tiny shoot was soft, the roots shallow and thin as thread. I planted it and within a couple months, it had grown into a shrub with fragrant white trumpet flowers that opened at night and wilted in the next day's heat. Day after day, I watched them, full of wonder at their rhythms of rising and falling. I noticed that in the place of each withered flower, a spiky seed pod formed holding dozens of seeds. When the pod was cracked open or crushed, the seeds were released and scattered along the ground where they burrowed. All winter long, the seeds waited in darkness, silently storing their strength. When spring came, their countless shoots shattered through soil. Each year, the moonflowers multiply. They come back stronger. They take new ground.

What, then, is the secret of Advent? The present darkness is not a tomb. It is a door.

## Prayer

*Meet us here, O God of winter and waiting,*
*O God who struggles with us and kindles*
*our hope.*
*Come in all your splendor and suffering.*
*Comfort all who mourn.*
*Let all who are crushed rise into the blooming of*
*a new and better world.*
*Teach us to channel our collective lament,*
*longing, and love*
*into a force that can raise the devastations and*
*rebuild the ruined cities.*
*Show us that the darkness around us and*
*within us is a door. It is soil and we are seed.*
*Show us that we are wick and your spirit is*
*flame. Alone, we flicker. Together, we blaze.*
*Amen.*

# Practice

Lindsey's holy longing shows up bodily: groans and heart swell, weak knees. Find a comfortable seat and a few quiet minutes. Bring your attention to your breath to center in your body and spirit. Ask, "What is my holy longing?" As the answer rises up, notice what your body is feeling. How is the Spirit in you groaning for reconciliation? In a change of pulse or breath? Through tension in your neck or tiredness in marching feet? Today hear the prayer of hope from your heart, mind, and body.

# Bio

Lindsey Krinks is a street chaplain, educator, homeless outreach worker, housing rights organizer, and cofounder of Open Table Nashville, an interfaith homeless outreach nonprofit. She writes about her work on her blog Dry Bones Rattling (drybonesrattling. wordpress.com) and can be found in tent cities, washing feet on the streets, marching for social and economic change, and foraging for native herbs and plants. She is the author of the forthcoming book *Praying with Our Feet* (Brazos Press, 2021).

---

1. George Eliot, *Romola* (1862; New York: Penguin, 1996), 549.

# December 20

## Robyn Henderson-Espinoza

# Text for the Day

*A man named John was sent from God. He came as a witness to testify concerning the light, so that through him everyone would believe in the light. He himself wasn't the light, but his mission was to testify concerning the light.*

*John 1:6-8*

# Reflection

In a world where we are often sidelined for our imaginations, I think it's good to return to John's practice of testifying to the light.

The light for the Gospel of John helps us have an imagination of a container for truth, but because of systemic violence perpetuated by multilayered oppressions, the truth is skewed. Our political theater has created policies that undermine our efforts to create sustainable communities; and the police state, in the systematic execution of black and brown bodies, has normalized violence as the mode of surveilling infractions and controlling bodies. This has created a great amount of social unrest, and as a result, our communities are far from the light and unable to testify to any notion of the light.

In the search for truth, goodness, and beauty, which are all forms of the light in the Gospel of John, this Advent we have a chance to lean into the politics of possibility by relearning our own testimony and relearning the light that has been hidden from us as a result of violence and oppressions.

To relearn the light, we must also recalibrate to the light. This move toward the light is grounded in the deep intention of unmasking the truth, so that we can see more clearly. Only when we are able to see more clearly and begin to understand the contours of darkness that have prevented our welcoming of the truth can we begin to return to any notion of the light. Once we return to the light, we can begin to testify to the light.

The good news is that the Gospel of John reminds his readers that the person sent from God, John the Baptist, came to testify to the light, which tells us that there is a connection to the light for John the Baptist. Recognizing this entanglement of humanity with God as an inherent reality helps us lean into the practice of returning to the light, supporting our process of testifying to the light. Because we all have a divine spark and are all entangled with all that is God, this helps us harness the truth of the light, so that we can devise practices and politics that support the infrastructure that is required for us to invest in testifying to the light.

As we keep watch this Advent for the light that is inside all of us and the light that surrounds all of us, may we commit to uncovering all that steals light from us so that we can see and understand more clearly and so that we can help midwife a larger beam of the light. The work of uncovering all that steals light from us is the work of eradicating all forms of violence, despite its normalization, and leaning into a posture where we all are birthing shalom and allowing for Emmanuel to be present in all things.

## Prayer

*Light of life, be bright within me, be bright
around me.*

*Claire Brown*

## Practice

Today, light a candle as a form of prayer. Watch as the flame catches on the wick with fits and starts and flickers. As the light burns, it will recalibrate, change, settle. May the truth of this recalibration in the candle's burning remind us of our own need to shift and find our fuel, be challenged to better seeing and clearer light, and be open to the Spirit's transformation as we keep watch and witness.

# Bio

Robyn Henderson-Espinoza is the author of *Activist Theology* (Fortress, 2019). Robyn draws on their identity and heritage as a Transqueer Latinx in everything they do. As an anti-oppression, anti-racist, nonbinary Trans*gressive Latinx, Robyn takes seriously their call as an activist theologian and ethicist to bridge together theories and practices that result in communities responding to pressing social concerns. Robyn sees this work as a life-orienting vocation, deeply committed to translating theory to practice, and embedded in reimagining our moral horizon to one which privileges a politics of radical difference. Robyn has a PhD in constructive philosophical theology from the University of Denver.

# December 21

## Shane Claiborne

# Text for the Day

*The LORD God's spirit is upon me,*
*    because the LORD has anointed me.*
*He has sent me*
*    to bring good news to the poor,*
*    to bind up the brokenhearted,*
*    to proclaim release for captives,*
*        and liberation for prisoners,*
*    to proclaim the year of the LORD's favor*
*        and a day of vindication for our God,*
*    to comfort all who mourn,*
*    to provide for Zion's mourners,*
*    to give them a crown in place of ashes,*
*    oil of joy in place of mourning,*
*    a mantle of praise in place of discouragement.*
*                                            Isaiah 61:1-3*

# Reflection

A few years ago, I remember a pastor friend telling me they tried something a little different for their Christmas services. Instead of the usual holiday décor, they brought a bunch of manure and hay into the sanctuary and scattered it under the pews so the place would really smell like the manger where it all began. I laughed as he described everyone coming in, in all their best Christmas attire, only to sit in the rank smell of a barn.

They even brought a donkey in during the opening of the service that dropped a special gift as it moseyed down the aisle. Folks looked awkwardly at each other. Some were offended, some snickered, and some left. But for those who stayed . . . it was something like they'd never seen before. It was one of the most memorable services they've ever had.

They were reminded of the real meaning of Christmas—God entered the crap.

Jesus was born in a dirty manger because there was no room in the inn. God came into the world as a refugee, born to a teen mom who couldn't afford the more expensive offerings often presented in the temple at the birth of a new child.

As Jesus was born, the Gospel of Matthew tells of a terrible massacre that occurred, an unspeakable act of violence as King Herod slaughters children, hoping to kill Jesus, which the church remembers as the massacre of the "Holy Innocents."

Perhaps the original Christmas was marked more with agony and grief than with the glitz and glamour of the shopping malls and parades. From his birth in the manger as a homeless baby, until his brutal execution on the Roman cross, Jesus reminds us that God is with us.

That's what Emmanuel means, "God with us." God is with us in the struggle to survive, amid the throes of poverty, in the fight for freedom, in a world full of violence. Jesus' coming to earth is all about a God who leaves the comfort of heaven to join the struggle here on earth. God is with us.

Jesus did not just come to help immigrants and refugees; he came *as* a refugee. Jesus is the most incredible act of divine solidarity the world has ever known.

Let's remember this Christmas that the Savior we celebrate was born into the crap. He couldn't care less whether we say Merry Christmas or Happy Holidays. He's much more interested in our getting dirty in the trenches than decorating the temple. What Jesus cares about is how we care for the most vulnerable people on earth—the widows and orphans, the immigrants and refugees, the sick and the homeless.

The world we live in, like the world Christ lived in, is ravaged with violence and poverty. But the good news is that a Savior is born. He has come to preach good news to the poor and to disturb the rich. He has come to cast the mighty from their thrones and to lift up the lowly. He has come to bind up the brokenhearted and proclaim freedom to the captives. He has come to remind us that God is with us—if we are with the poor.

## Prayer

*Jesus, the impoverished refugee,*
*you showed up in the mess,*
*and the crap,*
*and the stench.*
*You told us to look for you in prison,*
*on the streets,*
*among the thirsty and hungry,*
*naked and alone,*
*those who are sick.*
*And yet sometimes, we do all we can*
*to avoid every one of those*
*places and people.*
*Convict and compel us to stop trying*
*to get you to show up where we want to go,*
*and instead start showing up where you told us*
*you would always be.*
*Amen.*

*Michael T. McRay*

## Practice

For some people, the last few days before Christmas are stuffed with gatherings, errands, and last-minute purchases. The parties and busyness are just too much.

For others, they are filled with end-of-the-year work stress, loneliness, or painful seasonal reminders we'd rather do without. The isolation and pressure are just too much.

Today, wherever you are, take a moment to pause. Remember that God is here. God is with us. Say it out loud: "God is here. God is with me." Whatever is going on, that is abundance for this moment.

## Bio

Shane Claiborne is a best-selling author, renowned activist, sought-after speaker, and self-proclaimed "recovering sinner." Shane writes and speaks around the world about peacemaking, social justice, and Jesus, and is the author and coauthor of numerous books including *Beating Guns*, *The Irresistible Revolution*, *Jesus for President*, and *Executing Grace*. He is the visionary founder of The Simple Way in Philadelphia, and cofounder of Red Letter Christians. His work has been featured in Fox News, *Esquire*, SPIN, the *Wall Street Journal*, NPR, and CNN.

# December 22

J. J. Warren

# Text for the Day

*When the angel came to her, he said, "Rejoice, favored one! The Lord is with you!" She was confused by these words and wondered what kind of greeting this might be. The angel said, "Don't be afraid, Mary. God is honoring you. Look! You will conceive and give birth to a son, and you will name him Jesus. He will be great and he will be called the Son of the Most High. The Lord God will give him the throne of David his father. He will rule over Jacob's house forever, and there will be no end to his kingdom."*

*Then Mary said to the angel, "How will this happen since I haven't had sexual relations with a man?"*

*The angel replied, "The Holy Spirit will come over you and the power of the Most High will overshadow you. Therefore, the one who is to be born will be holy. He will be called God's Son. Look, even in her old age, your relative Elizabeth has conceived a son. This woman who was labeled 'unable to conceive' is now six months pregnant. Nothing is impossible for God."*

*Then Mary said, "I am the Lord's servant. Let it be with me just as you have said." Then the angel left her.*

Luke 1:28–38

# Reflection

It was Christmas break. My first semester of college had ended, and I was on the train home from New York City. Thick snowflakes had begun to fall. As I left the station, my father was there to greet me. We shared a strong relationship. We talked about everything: faith, relationships, dreams, the latest Starbucks drink. But as I climbed into his blue truck that night, I was quiet.

After a few minutes, he looked at me and said, "You're not telling me something. What's up?"

"Nothing," I said, staring out the window. "Just tired, I guess."

But he asked again. "Come on J, you always talk to me. What is it?"

My chest became tight, and I could feel a headache coming. For some reason, I was nervous about what he might say next. After another moment of silence, he said, "You know J, if you're gay that's OK."

In that second, all the tension and fear that had gathered in my shoulders released. I breathed deeply. I opened my phone and timidly showed my father a photo of me with my first boyfriend by a Christmas tree. He smiled and said, "You two look good together." It was a good beginning.

Mary, a young girl from Nazareth, was going about her daily life when suddenly she was confronted with something unexpected. The angel Gabriel told Mary that she would give birth to God's son. No one would ever see her the same way, and she might be rejected by those who didn't understand what God was doing. She was afraid, but the angel was sent to encourage her.

I connect to what I imagine Mary must have felt. I did not plan on coming out to my father or my entire family that Christmas, but a moment of great fear turned into a surprise of joy and anticipation. I feared that my family would not understand, or that they would just see me as different. But this is not what happened. It took a while for them to understand, but they accepted me, and I showed them grace as well.

As we approach Christmas, think about the Marys around you, or the queer kid with a secret. Who is carrying fear and uncertainty about what is to come? What does it mean to be surprised and overwhelmed by the uniqueness of one's identity? The angel Gabriel made a comforting appearance, and my father's face melted into a smile at the train station that Christmas. Today, where are the comforters when comfort seems impossible? Who comes to say, "Do not be afraid"?

Let's be this for one another. Be the voice of encouragement. Be companions of compassion and bringers of joy in unexpected places.

Sometimes acceptance is the one great impossibility. May such an impossibility come to life every day, and may it start with us. This Christmas season, let us offer this simple gift.

## Prayer

*God of impossible surprises,*
*the stories say*
*you led captives out of slavery,*
*used unlikely and marginalized people to*
*preach your message,*
*and even resurrected the dead.*
*They say you asked*
*a young girl*
*full of wonder*
*and fear*
*to bear a child.*
*And those stories say*
*that she said yes.*
*Help us have hope*
*in these impossible possibilities*
*so that we too will practice*
*liberation, inclusion, and resurrection.*
*Amen.*

*Michael T. McRay*

# Practice

Find a comfortable spot and take a couple of deeper-than-normal breaths. Ask yourself and Spirit, "What seems impossible today?" Maybe write down an initial thought or two. Then ask yourself and Spirit, "How is God making this impossibility possible?" Jot down thoughts if they come, but take that question with you through the day.

# Bio

J. J. Warren is a seminary student at Boston University School of Theology, a graduate of New York's Sarah Lawrence College, and a certified candidate for ordination in The United Methodist Church (UMC). After making an impassioned plea for the inclusion of LGBTQ+ persons at the UMC's top law-making assembly, J. J.'s speech went viral, and his advocacy has been covered by HuffPost, NBC, and WXXI Radio. His first book, *Reclaiming Church: A Call to Action for Religious Rejects*, will be available this February from Abingdon Press. J. J. now travels the world preaching a message of inclusion and forward progress. Stay connected to his movement at jjwarren.org.

# December 23

## Jeannie Alexander

## Text for the Day

*Mary said,*

> *"With all my heart I glorify the Lord!*
> *In the depths of who I am I rejoice in God*
> *my savior....*
>
> *He has pulled the powerful down from*
> *their thrones*
> *    and lifted up the lowly."*
> Luke 1:46-47, 52

# Reflection

Advent is the still point in the midst of war.

When powers and principalities target your body, or the body of your beloved, you know the agony of waiting and the necessity of hope. Advent is *ruah*, breath when you are otherwise drowning. It is this space of agony and hope where targeted bodies in prisons, homeless encampments, war zones, zones of capitalism, zones of racism, and zones of earth contamination and environmental assault hold tension in darkness and wait for the light.

Mary's words of hope are most surely a declaration of war as well, not as the aggressor but as one whose body is the target of a system that displaces and crushes, one whose body refuses to yield. The child growing inside of her is an act of resistance, and there is nothing meek or mild in her declaration of soul force. Systems hide their war on targeted populations through language and words such as incarceration, inmate, alien, super predator, relocation, profit margin, consumer, maximization, surplus labor, stock, development, and law and order, just to name a few.

Mary knows that Rome's justice offers no peace to her people, no security for her child. And so she holds space in the tension of resistance and clings to a hope that must surely look like madness in the face of empire. Giving birth to a child you know will be targeted by a system is an act of Advent. Living with purpose and intention in the face of an impossible life sentence is an act of Advent. Casting yourself and your family into an overcrowded boat to escape certain death for an uncertain future is an act of Advent.

John the Baptizer knows he is not the Messiah because Messiah is a movement, not the event of one human life. The continuous burning of hope and determination when you yourself will never reach the shore, will never see the promised land, may never be brought forth from exile, that continuous burning—that is the holy space, the slender margin, the borderland of Advent. Advent exists on the margins; the center has no need for such yearning and longing. It is the space that Advent occupies where the mighty will be brought low, and the axe will be put to the root. The small dim light of a single flame so tenderly cared for in Advent will become the fire to baptize the world.

Advent is the beginning of the end of domination. The mighty will be brought low, the walls will fall, the prisons will burn, deportation centers will crumble, those who are occupied will inherit the earth, and the hard-fought resistance will yield reconciliation. But all of this exists in the not yet, in the going forth. And so we keep going forth, daring not to die, birthing a new world, one Advent act of resistance at a time.

# Prayer

*Amma,*
*Make me an instrument of your fire.*
*Make me the breath in the lungs that scream for*
*justice.*
*Make me the tears on a mother's face holding*
*the body of her child scorched by war.*
*Make me a stone thrown at a tank.*
*Make me the key to open cell doors.*
*Make me the darkness to hide those fleeing*
*across a desert.*
*Make me the ocean that guides a refugee's boat.*
*Make me the scarf covering the face of Antifa.*
*Make me a vaccination in a free clinic.*
*Make me farmland never touched by chemicals.*
*Make me a guitar played by a prisoner's hands.*
*Make me a song of joy on a child's lips in Syria.*
*Make me, make me, just keep making me, God,*
*until there is nothing left to transform, and then*
*let me dissolve into you.*

# Practice

Like Mary, we feel the oppression of her people and the hope of the world in her body. But often we silence our body's lament or expectation.

Today we practice listening to that body wisdom and prophecy. Find a quiet, comfortable position. Close your eyes, and bring your attention to your breath. Notice the places where your body rests: on your chair, feet on the floor, hands in your lap. Let the rhythm of your breath lead your attention across your body, starting from your toes and feet to your legs and knees; your seat, belly, and back; your arms, hands, and fingers; your chest, shoulders, and neck; your face and head. Spend time noticing where pressure, tension, or relaxation are in your body without rushing past, judging, disciplining, and fixing. Let your body speak its Advent prayer.

# Bio

Jeannie Alexander is the director of No Exceptions Prison Collective, an urban farmer at Harriet Tubman House, a writer, poet, abolitionist, fierce activist, and lover of all things wild and untamed. She is the devoted partner and muse of Jacob Davis, a beloved daughter and friend, and soul force in the movement toward compassion and liberation.

# CHRISTMAS EVE

## Micky ScottBey Jones

## Text for the Day

*Mary said, "With all my heart I glorify the Lord! In
the depths of who I am I rejoice in God my savior.
He has looked with favor on the low status of his
servant. Look! From now on, everyone will consider
me highly favored because the mighty one has done
great things for me."*

*Luke 1:46-49*

# Reflection

I am a very verbal person. Sometimes I talk too much. In fact, the note in my otherwise stellar second grade report card was, "She is a good student, but she talks too much." So it's no surprise that pregnancy, birth, and motherhood, all seasons of life where there is much to process verbally or otherwise, increased not only the amount of my verbal expression but also, at times, the volume.

While waiting on the arrival of a child during three Advent seasons, my thoughts were often preoccupied with Mary.[1] Reading through the narratives of Jesus' birth, I wanted to know who she was. I wanted to know her backstory, her side conversations, her inner dialogues. Thanks to the writer of Luke and my practice of imaginative, contemplative prayer, my mind has scripted-in conversations between Mary and Elizabeth during her three-month visit. I've imagined the conversations she had with herself; I've imagined the doubt, anxiety, and excitement as she treasured all the words other people said about her baby and "pondered them in her heart" (Luke 2:19 NIV). I've wondered what her post-birth chatter was with Joseph when riding the oxytocin and adrenaline high that enters the room with a fresh-to-earthside baby.

I've wondered about neighborhood conversations where they whispered about bringing down the powerful, lifting up those who are low, filling up the bellies of the poor with good things, and sending rich people away without more.

I like to think she was a talker, like me.

I like to think she talked about these things with baby Jesus in her arms. She was his first teacher, his first source of news and direction. It was her words that bounced around his head as he grew into a young man and finally stood up in the temple to declare his mission to bring about those things his mama had always talked about.

He listened to his mama talk.

We are living in an era where action seems more important than ever. Words feel cheap and lots of talking can feel like a luxury. Yet, what we talk about while we wait—for a baby, for a child to grow, for a promise to be realized—is not just a filler in the story. Our talk—the words we craft, the stories we tell, the injustices we lament, the songs we sing—becomes our story and the stories of those to come.

What are you talking about while you wait? What conversations do you imagine during this time of Advent? Whose words have you heard as you waited on something to be birthed in your life?

# Prayer

*Mother, Father, Creator God,*
*Thank you for the words of our mothers in*
*righteousness—those who bring the feminine*
*energy of love and care and justice. May we*
*nurture the seeds planted in us during our times*
*of growth and waiting so that we might allow*
*them to nourish us when the time comes to be*
*born in a new way.*

# Practice

Find time today to answer these questions from Micky, whether with a friend or partner. "What are you talking about while you wait? What conversations do you imagine during this time of Advent? Whose words have you heard as you waited on something to be birthed in your life?" Let your answers be part of the larger story, a word of hope to others on the journey.

# Bio

Micky ScottBey Jones—the Justice Doula—accompanies people as they birth more love, justice, and shalom into our world. As a womanist, faith-rooted, contemplative activist, healer, and nonviolence practitioner, Micky supports faith leaders, activists, and everyday leaders in a variety of roles—speaker, writer, facilitator, and pilgrimage guide. Topics of expertise include creating brave space, movement chaplaincy, contemplative activism, healing and resilience, transformation through travel, sustainable leadership and community building. Micky has an MA in Intercultural Studies from NAIITS/Portland Seminary and is currently pursuing advanced studies in the Enneagram and writing a movement chaplaincy curriculum. She is the director of resilience and healing initiatives for Faith Matters Network based in Nashville, Tennessee. Connect with her at Faithmattersnetwork.org and MickyScottBeyJones.com.

---

1. I acknowledge that not every mother waits for their child through a pregnancy; some wait through adoption or other processes. I honor all routes to parenthood and share here my personal journey that did include physically carrying babies in my body, but I think Mary and her narrative have gifts for all, not just those who physically carry and birth babies.

# CHRISTMAS DAY

Sami Awad

## Texts for the Day

*They went quickly and found Mary and Joseph, and the baby lying in the manger. When they saw this, they reported what they had been told about this child. Everyone who heard it was amazed at what the shepherds told them.*

*Luke 2:16-18*

*Magi came from the east to Jerusalem. They asked, "Where is the newborn king of the Jews? We've seen his star in the east, and we've come to honor him."*

*Matthew 2:1b-2*

# Reflection

It is dear to my heart and soul to live in the city where the Prince of Peace was born. To reflect on the story of his birth not just as a historic event, but to fully be present to what it means to be a peacemaker today in the land where, even before he uttered a single word, the earth and heavens responded to him.

What does the birth of Jesus teach me today? This is the question in my heart every time this season approaches.

For me, the birth of Jesus was the birth of the vision of peace, and like any true vision of peace born in situations of power, domination, fear and resignation, there will always be a reaction. There will always be those who, out of curiosity, will come and see, question, reflect, become inspired, and go tell others of what they saw. These shepherds still exist in our lives today but after they leave we almost never hear of them again.

There will always be those who will bring gifts and blessings to the peacemakers, financial and other forms of supporting the work. These magi still exist in our lives today, and as great as their support is, the question is, what do they do beyond the gift giving?

Finally, there will always be those who will reject and fight us for our message of peace and justice that threaten their power and domination. These Herods still exist in our lives today. What makes the Herods different from the shepherds and magi is that until they give up their fight or are transformed, they will always be there to fight, reject, and persecute the peacemakers. These are the ones who stayed in the story throughout the life of Jesus, challenging him, attacking him and trying to undermine him in everything he said and did. The ultimate expression of their fear of his message of peace was in their killing the messenger, thinking that this will also lead to the death of the message as well.

As peacemakers, we should always be thankful and welcoming of all the shepherds and magi that have entered and continue to enter our lives. We have been blessed with people who want to learn, who want to share our experience with others, and who want to support our work and programs. However, we must not ignore those who are always present—the Herods who never give up on their desire to remain in power and thus persecute, undermine, or try to completely marginalize and destroy us.

It is comforting for us as peacemakers to focus our energy on those who like us, lift us up, and support us, but that is not why we exist. As peacemakers we are called to have the strength to stand in the face of those who persecute us. We are called to stand in faith, belief, and vision, knowing that our ultimate celebration is the healing and transformation of their hearts and souls.

# Prayer

*Jesus of Bethlehem,*
*your journey began in the womb,*
*like ours.*
*On this day, we remember how*
*your teenage mother birthed the Prince of Peace.*
*May we be more like your mother,*
*birthing into the world*
*more peace, justice, and love.*
*Because if our pain can bring*
*new life,*
*it may be worth it.*
*Amen.*

*Michael T. McRay*

## Practice

Today find a moment of quiet and grounding. Center yourself with a few deeper than normal breaths. Give thanks for the journey of Advent preparation and for the gift of Christmas.

As we enter the celebratory season of Christmas today, the twelve days of joy and honoring the radical peacemaking of God with us, remember the creche that Sami sketched out for us. Who are the shepherds that you can teach, encourage, and mobilize? Who are the magi and what gifts can you receive from them in this season of life and peace work? What or who is your Herod, and what is the work to challenge or transform this Herod?

In all these things, remember the work of preparation you have done through Advent, and like Mary, treasure the words of wisdom and moments of clarity in your heart.

## Bio

Sami Awad is the executive director of Holy Land Trust, a nonprofit committed to the principles of nonviolence. Holy Land Trust aspires to strengthen and empower the peoples of the Holy Land to engage in spiritual, pragmatic, and strategic paths that will end all forms of oppression. Sami works locally, through promoting and engaging in nonviolence, healing, and transformation work, and globally, through visiting and speaking in different countries, communities, and political and religious organizations all around the world. Sami is married to Rana Awad and together have three beautiful girls, Layaar, Larina, and Lorian.

# Using *Keep Watch with Me* with Groups

People of faith and goodwill who keep watch for God's work in the world—those who bear active witness—can never undertake this call alone. We are connected to a great cloud of witnesses, as the writer of Hebrews put it (12:1). We are part of a legacy of all who've come before and work alongside us now to create more peace and justice in the world. It's crucial to seek out those witnesses through time and space and to find stories and figures that inspire us regardless of how near or far they are from us in history and context.

It is especially important to find those like-minded folks that are available for you to regularly connect with as spiritual companions. While the work of peacemaking can be lonely, requiring the courage to lift a rare voice in a world full of violence and chaos, it is work that is best done in community. *Keep Watch with Me: An Advent Reader for Peacemakers* connects you to people and communities around the world, receiving the gift of others' stories and wisdom for your own life and work. We hope that encountering these watch keepers, their stories, and their communities will lead you back to those people around you and help you rediscover your own stories and contexts.

In the spirit of keeping watch together, we hope that these suggestions for group study can be adapted for your context to provide meaningful engagement with the readings in your community. The guide is intended for folks who will gather to discuss the Advent reader at least on a weekly basis. It might be through a digital platform, a faith community small group, or with friends or family.

Advent is a meaningful but very brief and often very busy season. If you can make time to discuss the readings more than once, this practice should create more grounding, connection, and transformation for you and your conversation partners. The practice also helps keep your heart and mind in an attitude of journeying through the days toward Christmas. The guide includes prompts for discerning our own calls to keep watch, approaching the spiritual practices in a community, exploring diverse and new voices and reflection, and connecting *Keep Watch with Me* to the worship and experience in our faith communities and traditions.

# Keeping Watch in Community

The activists, authors, clergy, organizers, educators, and others who have contributed to *Keep Watch with Me* are shaped by the ways that they keep watch for God's work in the world. They are also defined by the ways they witness the tension between working for peace in the midst of brokenness and anticipating God's restorative wholeness. Many of these contributors are in occupations and roles that align with the work of peace and justice, but all people of faith, no matter their vocations, are called to keep watch for and join in with God's presence and love in the world.

As you meet with others to reflect on this Advent journey, your conversations can become creative incubators for discerning your call to the work of peace or recognizing those places in your life where you are already participating in the transformative divine presence. Not only do we become aware of this call in our lives by expanding our sense of what it means to keep watch and make peace but also through reconsidering the contexts of our lives. What environment surrounds us? What is our neighborhood? Who around us is in need of peace and reminders of God's loving presence? Who around us is in need of advocacy and partnership for their well-being in the world? Who around us is a potential partner in peacemaking and watch keeping? Start with the community nearest to you as you wonder about how to keep watch in community.

Questions for discussion:

- How do you spend your days, and what makes you feel most alive?
- What is your work of peace and justice, and how can you broaden your view of this work in your life?
- How have you kept watch this week?

# Spiritual Practices in Community

For many of us, the spiritual practices in this book are new, and many may challenge us as we broaden our ideas of prayer and connecting with God. Again, no spiritual practice, no way of praying, is one-size-fits-all. While we encourage you to try new approaches and be open to the invitations of each practice, we also affirm the different experiences and comfort levels of readers. If a practice doesn't resonate with you, move on, or perhaps revisit it at a later time. If one is particularly meaningful or illuminating for you, make note and return to it again.

If you like to journal, add written reflection to your daily reading and practice as a form of prayer in this Advent and beyond. This can serve to deepen your connection to the material, but also gives record that will help you bring your solitary reading and prayer into conversations with others.

Take your reactions as well as your thoughts and experiences of the practice to your conversation partners. Review the week's offerings together. Note where the Spirit was particularly speaking in a prayer or practice or where you felt at the edge of your comfort zone. Notice together where aversion or longing occurred as you read and prayed. Without judgment for difference in experience, wonder together at how different ways of praying and reflecting offer spiritual nourishment to some people and not others. Share previous experiences of faith formation or encounter with the divine that might be shaping how you approach the prayers and practices in this reader.

Questions for discussion:

- Which prayers or practices stood out to you this week?
- Which spiritual practices were new to you?
- How have you connected with God and yourself this week?

# Keeping Watch Across Difference

*Keep Watch with Me* features writers from many different sexual orientations, races and ethnicities, gender identities, citizenships, educational and professional backgrounds, theological and political views, religious affiliations, and vocations. The book is rich in its reflections, challenges, and questions because of this wide variety of voices. Praying, learning, and reading faith and theology from multiple social locations and stories offers us a fuller understanding of God. All people are made in the image of God, and the differences of story, culture, personality, and perspective we bring to our faith help expand and nuance our sense of God's image.

Historically, Christian religious traditions have not been outwardly led by such a diverse array of leader and voices, and many continue to silence, marginalize, and exclude women, LGBTQ+ folks, and people of color from leadership and theological authority. If this is true in your experience, perhaps this reader offers you the opportunity to think more broadly about people's experiences of God, and to think more broadly about who has authority to speak into your life about God. A trusted group is a great place to explore some of the tensions and openings we encounter in ourselves as we are exposed to new theological voices. Spend some time reflecting with the group about what perspectives you're used to hearing, and what perspectives in this reader might be new for you.

Questions for discussion:

- Who are the people who have most shaped how you think about God?

- Are there perspectives and voices in this book
  that are new to you?
- How do you think about differences in how a
  diverse group of people thinks about faith, God,
  and the work of peacemaking?

## Keeping Watch in Worship

Advent has ancient roots as a season in the Christian church that is marked by penance and preparation for the coming celebration of Jesus' birth. Sacred music of the season reflects the tension of anticipation, our need for God's help, and joy at God's coming. Some Christian traditions mark the passage of the season with weekly themes of hope, love, joy, and peace. Traditions that use the lectionary, a listed schedule of Scripture readings used across denominations, journey from Old Testament prophetic texts of messianic coming and apocalypse to the Gospel narratives about the birth of Jesus.

Christmas Eve service is one of the two best attended of the church year, but for those of us who are part of communities of faith, intentionally walking through the weeks with our worship and corporate prayer can bring a deeper level of meaning to the festivities of Christmas. If you claim a particular faith tradition, do some research into what your Advent practices are and how your community worship reflects the themes and theology of this season. Connecting your reading, prayer, and practice from *Keep Watch with Me* to the reading, prayer, and practice of a faith community might give you the opportunity to create more theological connections as the two experiences inform one another and help you learn more about your traditions and those of others.

Questions for discussion:

- What are the practices and traditions around Advent and Christmas in your faith tradition?
- Where do you see the readings connect to this week's corporate worship and prayer?
- How do the readings diverge from your experience of corporate worship and prayer?

*Claire Brown*
*January 2019*
*Chattanooga, Tennessee*

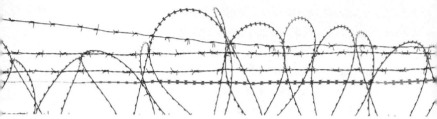

# Keeping Watch Together

*It is in the shelter of each other*
*that the people live.*
*—Irish saying*

There was a time when I entered maximum security prison units to try to keep men from harming themselves. I was a volunteer chaplain, and men in these units were locked in solitary confinement twenty-three hours per day, seven days per week. At the end of each day, I would walk across the sidewalk, through metal gates and steel doors, back to the chaplain's office. Sometimes I prayed old monastic prayers; sometimes I said nothing along the way.

In the office, the head chaplain, Jeannie (December 23), her two clerks—Jacob (December 6) and Tony (December 12)—and the assistant chaplain, Kayla, would sit with me and remember the day. We would tell stories, process, strategize, mourn, laugh, and cry. One day, Jacob said to me, "Mike, the light is disappearing from your eyes. This place is sapping your soul." And he was almost right. There *were* days when the place, the pain, and the people were all too much, when quitting to retreat into comfort and convenience beckoned me like Sirens. And on many of those days, I would have given in if I hadn't found shelter in the company of those four. We persevered by holding on to each other.

This Advent, we've invited you to see differently. Advent today is often a season of joy as we anticipate Christmas. We wait with joy because we know Christmas is coming every December 25. It never changes. But those who waited for Christ back then waited in faith, not certainty. They had to hope. And hope can be painful, fearful, vulnerable, and full of risk.

Today, we too must hope. We too must live in faith. We pray for the advent of justice. We yearn for more peace and less persecution. Sometimes we say, *Nothing will change until Jesus comes again.* And those words guarantee the world keeps burning. They let us off the hook because if only God can save us, what use is our hard work?

But what if God is waiting for us? What if God needs us because God is unwilling to do it alone? What if we—doing the good work God has already called us to—can help heal the world by healing our own corners of it? Our stories, our songs, our service, our shelter, and our sincerity may be the very things that welcome the world we long for.

This is where we need one another. The men in solitary confinement needed me to stay vigilant to their needs and humanity; I needed my friends to keep watch for mine. In the shelter of each other, we fanned the flames of hope that a better tomorrow was possible. We refused to abandon our call to create glimpses of heaven in the very halls of hell. That which we await is not yet fully here, and so we keep watch, holding fast to those we love so we don't buckle beneath the weight of the world's pain. We cannot allow ourselves to become paralyzed by the deluge of grief around us. Our call is simple: Do justice. Love mercy. Walk humbly. As the Pirkei Avot counsels us gently, we do not have to complete the work, but neither may we abandon it.[1]

Advent has come and gone again. We watched, we waited, and we worked, longing for a better world, believing one is possible. Indian author Arundhati Roy once said, "Another world is not only possible, she is on her way. On a quiet day, I can hear her breathing."[2]

Let us keep watch for this world together. Let us work for this world together. And on the days when we think it's all in vain, let us keep quiet, so that the sound of her breathing might stir us once again.

*Michael T. McRay*
*January 2019*
*Nashville, Tennessee*

---

1. The Pirkei Avot is a compilation of ethical sayings passed down to the rabbis.

2. Arundhati Roy, *An Ordinary Person's Guide to Empire* (Boston: South End, 2004), 86.

# Acknowledgments

### Claire and Michael

This reader would not exist were it not for you, the reader. We thank you first. And we express our tremendous gratitude to the nearly six thousand people from sixty countries who signed up to read the first version of this resource on Michael's blog for Advent 2017, and to the 1,500 of you who joined the Facebook discussion group to form a global community of peacemakers and encouragers. Your passion for this project directly led to the publication of this book.

We are indebted as well to the generosity of our extraordinary contributors, both to the original online Advent reader and to this publication: Whitney Kimball Coe, Shantell Hinton, Becca Stevens, Jacob Davis, Jarrod McKenna, Mark Charles, Brian Ammons, Pádraig Ó Tuama, Nontombi Naomi Tutu, Tony Vick, Gareth Higgins, Charles Strobel, Brittany Sky, Tarek Abuata, Justin Coleman, Ashley McFaul-Erwin, Lindsey Krinks, Robyn Henderson-Espinoza, Shane Claiborne, J. J. Warren, Jeannie Alexander, Micky ScottBey Jones,

Sami Awad, and Jennifer Bailey, Brian McLaren, Doug Pagitt, and Marie Howe. Thank you for your stories, your wisdom, and your willing hearts.

Our immense thanks to the good people at Abingdon Press, specifically Maria Mayo and Susan Salley, for bringing *Keep Watch with Me* into print with your advocacy and enthusiasm.

## Claire

I give particular thanks for Austin, my partner and biggest encourager, and to the communities at the Shalem Institute and Vanderbilt Divinity School, without whose forming voices of wisdom, presence, and passion this project would not be possible.

## Michael

I am thankful to my wise and wonderful wife, Brittany, who supports all my many projects, makes the world better through her own essential work, and has patience in her heart for an Enneagram 3 like me.

To my cocurator, Claire—I am grateful. From the moment you said to me, "What if we published an Advent reader on your blog?" we've taken a remarkable journey together on this project. My deep thanks to you for your collaboration and craft. It's been a delight to work alongside you.

To all peacemakers who have formed me—in Palestine, Israel, (Northern) Ireland, South Africa, Rwanda, prisons, and beyond—I offer thanks. Many of you are in this book; many are not. But your work and witness still shape me.

CPSIA information can be obtained
at www.ICGtesting.com
Printed in the USA
FSHW010836191119

9 781501 876332